# Liverpool: World Waterfront City

# 利物浦：世界级的滨水城市

# Liverpool: World Waterfront City

 cities500

ISBN 978-1-905547-07-4

*Cities500 International Publishers*
Vice-President and Publisher: Guy Woodland
Editor-in-Chief: Lew Baxter

Editing & Writing: Lew Baxter
Principal photography: Guy Woodland
Front cover design: Paula Hutchinson
Proof reading: Judy Tasker
Printed and bound: Vivapress SL, Barcelona, Spain
Additional writing as credited - see essays

First published in 2008 by Guy Woodland
in association with *Cities500*
as a *21st Century Cities* publication

*Studio and Office:*
No 2 The Old Stables, Charles Road, Wirral, CH47 3BP. UK
*Tel:* + 44 (0) 151 632 3280
*Skype:* +44 (0) 151 324 1273
*e.mail:* info@cities500.com

www.cities500.com

*This wonderful 'bird's eye' view was taken by Liverpool-born photographer Hal Mullin whose forte was aerial and shipping photography. He was flying in a small Cessna 172 above this veteran twin-engined, propeller-driven Douglas DC3 Dakota as it seemingly effortlessly winged its way over the Albert Dock in 1988.*

This book is dedicated to the memory of

## Hal Mullin

Liverpool Photographer 1944–2008

# Chapters & Essays

Acknowledgments 9
Foreword by The Duke of Westminster 13
Foreword by Francesco Bandarin 15
Foreword by Michael Heseltine 17
Foreword by Professor Phil Redmond 19
Overview by Lew Baxter 21

Chapter 1 – Crosby to Seaforth 25 – 44

Michael Brown 34 – 36
Peter Elson 40

Chapter 2 – Seaforth to North Docks 45 – 58

Michael Heseltine 46 – 47
Fred O'Brien 50
Nick Earlam 54

Chapter 3 – North Docks to Pier Head 59 – 78

Neil Scales 66 – 68
Jim Gill 76

Chapter 4 – Pier Head and Three Graces 79 – 162

Peter Mearns 84 – 86
Peter Grant 92
John Belchem 98 – 100
Steve Burnett 108 – 110
Andrew Harrison 114
Phil Redmond 118 – 120
Jack Stopforth 130 – 132
Tony Storey 138
Steve Maddox 142 – 143

Judith Feather 148
Kerry Brown 152
Martin Clarke 156

Chapter 5 – Albert Dock 163 – 190

Andrew Morris 168 –169
Frank Robotham 172 – 174
Cathy Roberts 178
Stephen Broadbent 182
Susan Hanley–Place 186 – 188

Chapter 6 – Urban Reflections 191 – 208

Christoph Grunenberg 196
Peter Morton 200 – 202
Victor Ashley 206

Chapter 7 – South Docks to Otterspool 209 – 220

David Fleming 214 – 215

Chapter 8 – Otterspool to Hale 221 – 238

Zeng Zhi Gao 224
Louise O'Brien 230 – 232
Mike McCartney 236

# Introduction & Acknowledgements

THERE was a mild dilemma about publishing this book as Liverpool has been in a state of flux in these early years of the 21$^{st}$ century. The views and skyline of the waterfront and the city alter almost by the month. It could never be up to date.

Then we realised that maritime cities like Liverpool are constantly changing – and this has been the case for centuries. Any time or any age would never allow a complete and final picture.

The book is thus defined as a relatively contemporary pictorial record of Liverpool as a world waterfront city – with the emphasis on waterfront, and in particular as Liverpool was inscribed into UNESCO's World Heritage lists in 2004 for what is termed its 'Maritime Mercantile City' legacy.

The photographs have been carefully chosen to show how the light and mood over Liverpool and its river is a never–ending source of surprise. The scene changes swiftly from dark and sombre to bright and breezy, and the images capture the activities, day and night and in all seasons and weathers. The waterfront is never boring or mundane and it has enchanted and engrossed generations of people.

We have undertaken this journey from north of the city up at Crosby and sweeping down past Royal Seaforth Dock – at the heart of today's Port of Liverpool – and towards the grand 'trinity' of buildings at the Pier Head that is the natural focal point. It is acknowledged as one of the most thrilling sights from the bridge or deck of an approaching ship. Then we cast our eye further upstream along the banks of the mighty river Mersey – on both the Liverpool and Wirral sides – towards its widest point at Hale shoreline.

All waterfronts have a dynamism and an emotional effect on people and in this book we are delighted that a number of esteemed essayists have contributed their observations and reflections on what the river and the waterfront mean to them – as well as the city of Liverpool in general. In terms of the book's flow, the essays are not specific to the chapters, or indeed in any order of preference or priority. They act as 'bridges' between the photographs, both elements meshing to create what we feel is a panoramic and passionately told story.

Many people have contributed to this book on various levels; their enthusiasm and support have been essential and welcome.

As usual we acknowledge Michael Brown from Liverpool John Moores University who has demonstrated continuing faith in our publishing endeavours, as has Peter Mearns from the Northwest Regional Development Agency, and Neil Scales at Merseytravel who didn't hesitate when the idea was pitched at him; Andy Pomfret and Andrew Morris at Rathbones were also very upbeat. We would also like to thank Steve Burnett and Liz Romnes at Royal Liver Assurance; professors Drummond Bone and John Belchem at the University of Liverpool; Alexis and Phil Redmond – the city's 'Cultural Zsar' and an affable if canny dealmaker; Jack Stopforth at the Liverpool Chamber of Commerce; Eric Leatherbarrow and Frank Robotham at the Mersey Docks & Harbour Company – part of Peel Ports Group; Emma Degg and Steve Maddox at Wirral Borough Council; Andrew Lovelady at Ethel Austin Property Group, who was the first to support the project; Francesco Bandarin and Vesna Vujicic–Lugassy at UNESCO's World Heritage Centre in Paris; Lord Heseltine and Tracy Rodger at Haymarket Publishing; the Duke of Westminster; Chris Turner at Grosvenor Estates; Mark Thomas, editor of the *Liverpool Daily Post*; Mike McCartney in his capacity as a creative whiz and cultural ambassador for Wirral; Shonagh Wilkie and Janet Martin at Liverpool John Moores University; John Clayton at British Waterways; Jim Gill and Jonathan Clancy at Liverpool Vision; Henry Owen–John and Louise O'Brien at English Heritage; Peter Morton at Mersey Waterfront; David Fleming at National Museums Liverpool; Richard Edwards at Royal Liver Assurance; Christoph Grunenberg at Tate Liverpool; Kerry Brown from Chatham House and the Liverpool–Shanghai Partnership; Tony Storey for his encyclopaedic knowledge of the *QE2*; Nick Earlam and Elaine Daugan at Plexus Cotton; Andrew Harrison from the *Word* magazine for his fond memories of pigeons; Peter Grant and Cath 'Tugboat' Roberts for unstinting support and words that sparkle; Sue Hanley–Place for her dedication to phrases of passion; Fred O'Brien for his commitment to Liverpool's historical legacy; Peter Elson for gilded prose; Judith Feather for the River Festival and Tall Ships; Jonny and Jennie Baxter for continuing the sea–going wanderlust traditions; Zeng Zhi Gao for his long–standing friendship; Paula Hutchinson for encouragement and extremely useful suggestions; George and Henry Woodland for their roles as photographic assistants; Judy Tasker for 'literally saving the day' again; Victor and Paula Ashley for fabulous stories, and hospitality; and a host of others without whom our publishing projects would be merely wisps of unrealised ambition.

We hope that this book will be well received in Liverpool's sister port city of Shanghai, whose Bund has an equally striking – and similar – river front (*see essay page 152*). The book also highlights Liverpool's glorious World Heritage site at a time when such exiting developments as the *Waterfront Connections* project will link the Pier Head to the Albert, Canning and Salthouse docks creating a wonderful maritime park. This confirms that the waterfront is a sensational attraction for UK and international visitors alike.

# Celebrity Partners & Supporters

We would like to thank the following organisations and
individuals who have supported this project and without
whose assistance this would not have been possible.

Liverpool John Moores University

The Northwest Regional Development Agency

Merseytravel

Rathbones

Ethel Austin Property Group

The University of Liverpool

Phil and Alexis Redmond

Royal Liver Assurance

The Liverpool Chamber of Commerce

Mersey Docks & Harbour Company

Wirral Borough Council

English Heritage

# Foreword by The Duke of Westminster
## KG CB OBE TD CD DL

There is no doubt that the inscribing of World Heritage status on its historic waterfront was one of the most important decisions to affect Liverpool since King John bestowed Charter of the City eight centuries ago.

UNESCO's recognition underlines Liverpool's remarkable social, commercial and cultural renaissance in recent years, as well as acknowledging its epic maritime legacy.

Personally, I am delighted that Grosvenor has played a pivotal part in this revival with our Liverpool One project, arguably the largest and most dynamic regeneration construction programme in Europe so far this century.

Indeed, it has been hailed as one of the most important developments in Liverpool's long history and has transformed the city centre, as well as providing a gateway to the majestic waterfront.

Liverpool is now most definitely a 'world waterfront city' in every respect. Liverpool has regained its international stature and has further enriched its reputation.

**Eaton Hall
Chester
CH4 9ET**

## Foreword by Francesco Bandarin

## Director, UNESCO World Heritage Centre, Paris

The city of Liverpool played a fundamental and pioneering role in the Industrial Revolution that helped shape the Western world during the 19th century. This involved astonishing achievements in trade, technology and architecture which have left their traces in the historic docks and cultural buildings we can admire in the city today.

Liverpool was inscribed on the World Heritage List in 2004 for the major contribution it has made to worldwide industry and commerce through its maritime activities.

In addition to the many wonderful natural and cultural World Heritage sites inscribed on the List, it is important to include sites that embody the remarkable technical and architectural advancements that mark the modern age.

Humankind has had a greater impact on the environment in the last 200 years than in all of its previous occupation of the planet. The most impressive creations from this period are as significant, albeit in different ways, as any that came before them.

UNESCO is proud to count *Liverpool: Maritime Mercantile City* among the world's cultural heritage legacies. The city's outstanding universal value is embodied in its panoramic water-front and other key architectural features, and is reflected in its historical contribution to the major mercantile systems throughout the British Commonwealth.

For these reasons it remains a unique and integral part of our shared heritage, and I am confident that it will continue to be appreciated and protected for generations to come.

# Foreword by Michael Heseltine
## Lord Heseltine of Thenford

I have been associated with Liverpool for close on thirty years and am very proud of the title that was bestowed on me in the early 1980s as Minister for Merseyside. It was a time when Liverpool and the wider region didn't have that many friends either in government or business circles.

Yet, it was a very exciting, demanding and equally rewarding time. Indeed, I believed – and still do – that a new chapter of the city's history was being written. When I first took an interest and visited Liverpool in the late 1970s everyone believed it was finished. The city had endured such social, political and economic trauma: it was literally on its knees.

Yet, how wrong they all were. It has since become a 'national model of urban renaissance' and I have been constantly fascinated to see how it has developed in every aspect, and certainly over the last two decades in particular.

Of course, I have long been enchanted by its grand architectural heritage and the magnificence of the waterfront. I realised back in those early days of my commitment to Liverpool that the river Mersey is the lifeblood of the city but it had been turned into an open sewer. I determined to clean it up and to instil life back into the Albert Dock and the wider waterfront that also took in the International Garden Festival.

I am delighted that Liverpool is truly once more a 'World Waterfront City', enhanced by the UNESCO inscription as a World Heritage site. Who could ever have imagined that in the dark days of the past? Over the years I have come back to Liverpool many, many times and there is actually a part of me that will never leave this city.

HOUSE OF LORDS
LONDON SW1A 0PW

## Professor Phil Redmond CBE
## Chairman National Museums Liverpool
## and Chairman Merseyfilm

Everything I am is because of Liverpool. That may sound like a sentimental cliché but we are all products of where we come from. Our past informs our present and points to our future.

Liverpool is an old city with a relatively new heritage. 800 years old in 2007 yet its growth, decline and recent renaissance happened in the final quarter. It is a city built on the ebb and flow of tides. Those of its river. Those of the global rather than national or local winds of change. A city at the centre of nothing yet on the periphery of everything. A city on the edge.

This inevitably breeds a need for survival in the face of constant change. This in turn develops a feeling of distrust in the status quo and those who espouse it. This is why successive governments, of no matter what hue, have always found it difficult to engage with the local population. Centrally driven policies are seen as short–term palliatives akin to the opportunistic sales patters of the transient carpetbaggers of the past. Whether right or reasoned it is simply a fact of the people's shared heritage.

Ignore it and you will be ignored. Embrace it and you will be embraced, regardless of political hue. Respect returns respect. Understand that the city cultivates a disruptive, not obstructive culture. It is not about blocking change, but challenging the status quo by displacing old ideas and embracing the new.

Liverpool is a place that is always anticipating the turn of the tide. Looking for the new idea that will sweep away the old and usher in the new. That is its greatest strength. That is what formed me.

*An evocative photograph of Canning Dock adjacent to the Pier Head taken in 1908, a year after the Port of Liverpool Building was completed, a few years before the Liver Building began to rise from its foundations and eight years before the Cunard Building opened for business.*

# In Memory of Salty Old Sea Dogs

IT is probably the whiff of ozone and the tang of brine on the tongue that infuses an air of impertinent insouciance to folk who live in and around the world's great waterfront cities. The sea seems to nurture a feisty rebellion amongst populations that are tuned in to the hooting of ships' horns and the tales of jaunty mariners.

As an international maritime hub, Liverpool was well placed to nourish and foster other nationalities, its own rather anarchic nature shaped by people who arrived from far distant places, either *en route* to the New Worlds or seeking refuge and a home in the city that has rather impishly regarded itself as a 'place apart' in the overall view of the United Kingdom – a kind of breakaway state, epitomised in the confrontations between the city's Labour–run council and Margaret Thatcher's Tory government in the mid–1980s. The city even supported the Confederacy in the American Civil War of the 1860s.

From the seafaring heydays of the 19th and 20th centuries Liverpool has embraced foreign tastes in culture, food and fashion and is acknowledged for wonderful maritime exploits and, latterly, its musical and sporting legacies. But it is undoubtedly a maverick city, fiercely proud of a lippy – frequently dippy – reputation, boasting a widely varied, indomitable population. It is an explosive confection of passion and recklessness, moulded by wild yet often melancholy Celts from Wales, Scotland and Ireland, meshed to the fabulous racial mélange of its other myriad nationalities: a rare confederation of Chinese, Poles, Indians, Greeks, Jews and others from the Caribbean or Africa – many of the latter descendants of transported slaves or seamen; immigrant diasporas of numerous creeds, colours, creativity and chutzpah.

In the age of canvas–rigged sailing ships the river Mersey was pivotal to the emergence of Liverpool as arguably the most important seaport in the world. And in the wake of that briny fuelled fervour,

**LEW BAXTER**
*Editor–in–Chief*
*Cities500 International Publishers*

throughout the 20th century the awe–inducing Pier Head waterfront became a definition of the city's visual identity, an instantly recognisable icon both at home and abroad.

Yet there was more to the waterfront than this 'postcard' image. Until perhaps the late 1980s, along the miles of docks that sweep north, there were still pubs that hummed and throbbed to the fascination and association with foreign climes: establishments like the charismatic Caradoc, the Langton, the Bramley Moore, the Atlantic – the latter only two of a handful remaining of the 'old school boozers' – and Nell Flanagan's fabled Victoria Hotel, or the Dominion, with its life–size statue of a 19th century seafarer atop its roof, pointing seawards to the beckoning Atlantic ocean that drew ships and matelots into the gusts of the trade winds. Then south along Wapping the prow–shaped Baltic Fleet public house was formerly a haven for salty old sea dogs whose vessels sailed out of the Salthouse Dock, venturing into the freezing waters of northern Europe, or the doughty whalers that cruelly extracted riches from the giants of the deep. These often–intemperate taverns stitched the docks communities and the roving mariners together.

When, with chums, I operated the City Press news agency in the Port of Liverpool building throughout the 1980s, during political and economic storms that almost ran Liverpool aground, apart from covering stories that had national impact, we edited a series of publications focused on port and shipping related activities that while apparently local actually had a global relevance. We wandered at will around the waterfront and wrote about the lives and loves of people whose families and folklore were inseparably linked to the sea in some form or other: tales of both joy and hardship or of conflicts between bosses and unions that could set the docksides ablaze.

We encountered memorable characters like the mighty Dennis Kelly, leader of the port shop stewards who was relentless when defending 'the lads', and Jimmy Symes, an almost legendary union man on the docks; or the urbane James Fitzpatrick, the Dock Company's chief executive, and later Trevor Furlong whose avuncular appearance disguised a steely resolve.

I was utterly seduced by the functions of the port: the cobbled quaysides, the cast iron bollards, the bustling sheds in the boondocks; the smells of grain, oil, timber, molasses and rust, or the clatter of steel containers at Royal Seaforth dock, hauled by enormous overhead cranes aboard huge ACL vessels bound for Halifax or New York. It was an intoxicating time.

We regularly travelled up and down the river on fast pilot launches, or more leisurely aboard the floating crane Mammoth; or clambered aboard tugs and even occasional visiting Royal Navy ships, or peered into holds where below men toiled in the gloom and dust, the experience perhaps not so exotic for them.

The docks and their hinterland embodied a collective, now largely dispersed, of robust and generous people that were loyal to each other and their traditions. Wherever they are, hopefully they will endorse the new role for their beloved waterfront whilst raising a toast to its UNESCO–recognised heritage.

# Liverpool: World Waterfront City

*The* Red Arrow *display team performing over Liverpool Bay.*

# Chapter 1

*Crosby to Seaforth*

*The Isle of Man Steam Packet Company's catamaran* Snaefell *passes* HMS Ark Royal *at the entrance to the river Mersey in the summer of 2008.*

*The catamaran Snaefell heads towards the Pier Head after travelling from the Isle of Man.*

*A grand sight as the QE2 enters the Mersey in May 2004 and steams past the Perch Rock Lighthouse, towering 90 feet above the waves at New Brighton. The lighthouse began operations in March 1830 and finally fell victim to modern navigation technology in October 1973.*

The lighthouse at New Brighton – to a similar design as the famous Eddystone Lighthouse in Plymouth – stands silently flanked by Fort Perch Rock as a tanker heads back out to sea after unloading her crude oil cargo at Tranmere further up river.

# The Relationship Between City and River

### Professor Michael Brown CBE, DL

*Chief Executive and Vice Chancellor*
*Liverpool John Moores University*

LIVERPOOL is a city intricately shaped by the ebb and flow of the world's oceans. From the slave trade to World War II's transatlantic convoys, Liverpool's evolution has been defined by its relationship with the sea and, by extension, the cultures of the world.

These seafaring connections have also played a key role in Liverpool's recent renaissance. Beginning in the 1980s with the rebirth of the Albert and Princes Docks and continuing today with the expansion of the Port of Liverpool and the development of the Cruise Liner Berth at Pier Head, there is no doubting that after decades of decline, Merseyside's waterfront and maritime industry is back in the ascendance.

Liverpool John Moores University understands the importance of the relationship between the river and the traced back to 1892, with the formation of the Liverpool Nautical College, and today it caters for all levels of mariner training and education from deck officers to postgraduates.

The university's courses have an international reputation for innovation and its maritime teaching and research facilities are unrivalled anywhere in the UK. The Lairdside Maritime Centre is the only facility in Europe to have a 360° field of view ship simulator, plus an active tug escort simulator. This simulator training is so valued that mariners travel from all over Europe and beyond to use the facilities, navigating the potentially treacherous waters of the Mersey estuary and other ports around the world.

The 360° field of view ship simulator resembles a film set, with its high-tech lighting rigs and replica 'bridge' centre-stage. Once everything is activated it's like you've entered a virtual world, so realistic that if the weather turns nasty you can begin to feel a little queasy. Thanks to the highly detailed all-round views of locks and quaysides it's easy to forget that it's just a simulation. The simulator can be adapted to reflect the manoeuvrability and power of different ships, such as passenger ferries, container ships and tankers – exactly the type of ships that regularly travel up and down the Mersey. Thanks to the financial support of Shell and Svitzer, we have also installed bridge simulators for the two tugboats most commonly used on the river Mersey.

All three simulators can be configured to operate within one training scenario. For example, one bridge may be configured as a tanker, with the other two bridges configured as tugs. This allows everyone to train together and work through a series of 'what-if' scenarios in total safety. We know that simulation can't replace real experience, but well-planned and presented exercises can prepare the professional mariner for those once in a lifetime hazardous experiences.

The importance of such training becomes apparent when you consider that Shell's Tranmere Oil Terminal, on the south bank of the Mersey, handles up to 11 million tonnes of crude oil a year for the company's Stanlow Oil Refinery. Safety is paramount for Shell and the Lairdside Maritime Centre's ship simulators enable personnel to complete joint pilot and tug master training in a highly realistic but totally risk-free environment.

It's not just local sailors that benefit. Thanks to a major contract with the Saudi Ports Authorities, we are delivering a suite of training programmes and port simulation to its employees. We are delighted to be working with the Saudi Ports Authorities, which operate eight ports, including three major container terminals and two ship repair yards. These are some of the world's busiest and most important international ports. In the past two decades alone they have handled more than 1,300 million tonnes of imports and exports. This equates to 12,000 ships visiting Saudi ports every year – roughly one ship every 30 minutes. By working together we can

ensure their workforce continues to have the skills required by today's challenging maritime industry.

And it's not just the facilities that make our maritime courses so impressive. Experts in our Marine, Offshore and Logistics research group specialise in maritime technology and maritime operations, and are internationally recognised as experts in safety and risk assessment. We have forged industrial research collaborations with AMEC, Bibby Line, Shell, Lloyds Register and the Offshore Safety Division of the Health & Safety Executive. This combination of innovative research and close links to the maritime professions ensure that our curriculum and students are kept up-to-date with advances in technology and professional practice.

The offshore oil industry has to take into account the weather, naval architecture, buoyancy, mooring and anchoring techniques when planning its operations. Underwater exploration and the transportation of oil and gas to refineries and plants on land are highly technical, dangerous processes. Mistakes can be economically and environmentally damaging, and in extreme cases even cost human lives. Our ongoing research on topics such as risk and safety, electronic charts and navigation studies are helping to reduce these risks and, when combined with our close links to the maritime industry and regulatory bodies, this work is also helping to ensure that our maritime curriculum is kept up-to-date with advances in technology and professional practice.

The university also plays its part in encouraging and recognising outstanding contributions related to navigation and marine activities so important to the city. A few years ago, we conferred an honorary fellowship on the former merchant seaman, Sir Robin Knox-Johnston, who exemplifies our ethos: Dream, Plan, Achieve. The first man to sail single-handedly round the world non-stop, Sir Robin's achievements are underpinned by a fierce determination to succeed and traditional values such as self-reliance, teamwork and learning to pick yourself up after defeat.

Thanks to his passion for sailing, Liverpool has been the starting and finishing point for three Clipper Round the World yacht races. Organised by Clipper Ventures plc, which Sir Robin founded in 1995, these events not only attracted thousands of international visitors to the city, generating millions for the North West economy, but also helped reconnect the city with the river that has shaped its development.

Though it's over four decades ago since his ketch *Suhaili* sailed into Falmouth Harbour after 312 days at sea, it's not surprising that Sir Robin remains a truly inspirational figure. Never more so than when he kept an audience of some 1,000 people enthralled while he delivered one of the university's prestigious Roscoe Lectures on what it means to be a good citizen in the 21st century.

The university also finds ways of helping the public enjoy the facilities originally created to support maritime trade. The renaissance of the Albert Dock embraces much more than sailing ships and it is increasingly attracting a new kind of tourist to the city – the 'culture vulture'. Thanks to a unique partnership with the Albert Dock Company, we were able to establish a new art gallery there, providing an unusual platform for contemporary artwork produced by international and local artists as well as university students and staff. The gallery reflects our commitment to taking the art school out of the university and onto the streets of Liverpool, to provide easy access to the work and thus helping inspire future generations of creative talent.

While the region's coastline has provided inspiration for countless artists, these waters can be a deadly muse. Thanks to the efforts of its dedicated volunteers, the Royal National Lifeboat Institution has saved more than 137,000 lives since it was founded in 1824. Regionally, volunteers based at lifeboat stations in New Brighton, West Kirby and Hoylake have plucked countless people from the unpredictable waters of the Mersey and Dee estuaries and the Irish Sea. Without the RNLI, our coastal waters would be even more treacherous and we all have reason to be grateful for their unselfish and often dangerous endeavours.

The RNLI and the university share a commitment to training excellence. With only 10% of crews having a professional maritime background, training is the magic ingredient that turns these volunteers into lifesavers. We recognised the work of these volunteers and the importance of the RNLI with the presentation of a corporate award in recognition of the charity's vital search and rescue service, which has saved countless lives on the river Mersey, the North West coastline and beyond.

The Liverpool Pilots received similar recognition from us, a corporate award for their work in maintaining safe passage along the treacherous waters of the Mersey estuary. Ships entering or leaving the port of Liverpool not only have to negotiate forceful tides but also the shifting sandbanks of the Irish Sea and the Mersey. As safe channels are in constant flux, navigation is extremely dangerous and the presence of skilled pilots is absolutely essential. Thankfully, the Liverpool Pilots have operated an official pilot service for ships coming in and out of the river Mersey for the last 240 years.

In 2008, for the first time in 25 years, merchant navy cadet training returned to Merseyside, thanks to a new portfolio of nautical science and engineering courses offered by our university's Maritime Academy. Around 90% of all world trade – and 95% of UK goods – is moved by ships across the world's oceans, making the maritime industry essential to the global economy. Despite this the sector is experiencing a severe skills shortage, with demand for deck officers and engineers rising every year. By bringing professional maritime training back to Merseyside, the training and educational needs of this exciting profession can be addressed, giving the industry the highly skilled graduates it needs.

Liverpool's close affinity with the sea looks set to continue and, thanks to its outstanding teaching and research record, our university remains firmly at the helm of advances shaping the maritime industry in the 21$^{st}$ century.

'The university also plays its part in encouraging and recognising outstanding contributions related to navigation and marine activities so important to the city'

*The ghostly forms of the wind turbines on the river at Burbo Bank are like a scene from a Ridley Scott movie.*

The sun slowly sets over Crosby beach but Antony Gormley's truly visionary cast–iron figures never sleep. There are 100 ghostly larger than life sculptures, moulded from his own body, dotted along a two–mile stretch of the shoreline, few at first then gathering together as they reach the sea. They are part of a display the much–admired Gormley calls Another Place and which he installed in 2005.

# In the Premier League of World Rivers

**Peter Elson**
*Senior feature writer*
*Liverpool Daily Post*

WHEN bad King John officially declared Liverpool open for business, in 1207, he displayed an uncannily good grasp of geography. Some 200 miles away in London, unencumbered by satellite navigation, he alighted upon a river whose elements made it an ideal naval and mercantile haven to link England with Ireland, Scotland and Wales – thereby also, unwittingly, inventing the Scouse character.

Fast forward 800 years and, today, these topographical qualities remain unsurpassed as Liverpool once again welcomes the world's largest passenger liners and Royal Naval warships. This follows the inauguration of the cruise liner terminal by Cunard Line's *QE2* in October 2007.

After a gap of 34 years the regular appearance of these big ships, of a size and technology beyond the mental limit of any medieval mystic, finally anchors Liverpool's psyche once more, after decades adrift and unable to find any defining berth in the modern world.

This symbiotic relationship between man and Mersey is a near lifelong obsession for me. As a child, aboard the ferry *Royal Daffodil*, I recall a parade of black and white Isle of Man boats alongside the Princes landing stage, like a line of patient waiters. The flash of their orange–red funnels was the sole vibrant colour in the unremitting gloom of a morning sea–fret.

I fell for the city then, or thereabouts, and have still not recovered. The riverfront is much changed from when I watched *Empress of England* disembarking passengers and mail from Quebec and Montreal, a Furness Withy freighter batting up the river to Manchester or Holt's Blue Funnel flues stacked against the silhouette of Birkenhead.

Why should this watery affair continue? The Mersey is not ostensibly an attractive or friendly river; it runs very fast with an excessive tidal range, can be deceptively flat calm or cut up rough. It is usually brown or grey in colour, but at unexpected, magical moments, in the sharp light of a winter's afternoon, can turn the silver of lost treasure.

The Mersey is in the premier league of famous world rivers, with the Amazon, Ganges and Nile, but also is combined with being a great port, like New York and Venice. The biggest vessels can penetrate its centre and everyone's hearts beat faster on glimpsing their prows rearing up by the Royal Liver Building.

From lessons learned in Irish Sea trading, this town was built on risk–taking and inured to the vicissitudes of wind and tide. It was natural for its seamen to travel further in search of wealth, to Africa and America. Entrepreneurs such as Samuel Cunard grasped the potential of steamboats to launch transatlantic scheduled services. Alfred Holt saw Disraeli's purchase of the Suez Canal as a chance to open up the Far East – thereby bequeathing to Liverpool Europe's oldest Chinese community.

Liverpool's cornucopia of riches all stem from the sea, which is why much of its peerless mercantile architecture – recognised by World Heritage site status – pays obeisance in sculptural or decorative form to the sea.

After several decades' absence, I returned to Merseyside and I found my natural affinity rekindled. Serendipitously, there was a long–vacant unofficial role awaiting a spokesman–cum–soothsayer to channel the feelings of thousands of local Mersey waterfront–lovers, and also those around the world, through the website wonder of the *Daily Post*.

With rising anxiety, though, I have observed the boorish stampede for regeneration, denied to Liverpool for so long. This threatens the very essence of our striking waterfront, which draws countless tourists, who are desperately needed for our local economy. The dolt–headed indifference applies to the Mersey's priceless floating heritage, as I discovered when publicising through the *Daily Post* the preservation of irreplaceable ships.

*SS Manxman,* Europe's last steam turbine passenger ferry, *HMS Whimbrel,* the last surviving Battle of the Atlantic warship, and the Mersey Bar lightship, *Planet;* all deserve their place here, but are wilfully dismissed by local authorities and quango bodies who should know better, but simply do not care.

We are having better luck attempting to safeguard the Western Approaches HQ, from where the Battle of the Atlantic was directed, and the archive of Nicholas Monsarrat, Liverpudlian author of *'The Cruel Sea',* which is to be donated to the Liverpool Athenaeum club's library by his widow Ann.

Even so, the message that *HMS Whimbrel,* Western Approaches and the Monsarrat Archive together make an unmatchable international visitor attraction for Liverpool baffles the city's masters.

Yet, participating in the first–ever service, in 2008, commemorating the 800 souls who died when *SS Arandora Star* was sunk in 1940, or viewing the sensational Tall Ships' races event for the third time, also superbly staged here in 2008, you realise all is not lost.

The city's recent ceremony renewing its wedding vows to the sea is not masking a sham marriage.

A view across Crosby beach looking towards the now disused radar tower that first opened in 1974 at Royal Seaforth Dock. In fact, Liverpool was the first UK port to use radar in 1948.

# Chapter 2

*Seaforth to North Docks*

# Reflections on the Saving of a Mighty River

## Michael Heseltine discusses his affection for Liverpool with Lew Baxter

LORD HESELTINE

WHEN he talks about Liverpool there is a glowing glint in Michael Heseltine's eye. He unabashedly declares an ongoing affection for a city and a people that were, paradoxically, very much at odds with the political agenda that the Conservative government pursued throughout the 1980s.

As Secretary of State for the Environment, from 1979, he was despatched just 18 months later to contain and deal with the inner city riots that threatened the stability of the country. Liverpool, in particular, was in turmoil as Toxteth burned in the sultry summer of 1981.

Yet he had already earmarked Merseyside and Liverpool as the focal point for an urban regeneration programme that was to transform many cities and broke the taboos for public and private sector partnership in development schemes. It was very experimental and hugely controversial.

"Remember that the public and private sectors did not cooperate then. They were largely alien bodies shouting abuse at each other. Within a short period of time they were friends, working on joint schemes for a common purpose.

"It was very exciting and I felt we were making history. And, thanks to the Merseyside template, today this way of operating is the prevailing culture. It has changed the way in which urban development takes place and I regard Liverpool's resulting renaissance as remarkably rewarding."

Back in the 'dark days' he was very conscious that the area was in catastrophic economic decline and needed an injection of support and good will from central government. "Everybody told me that Liverpool was finished. They got it wrong."

He insists, though, that he did not predict the riots, as some have assumed. "I knew there were things wrong with Liverpool and Merseyside but the eruptions were a profound shock to me." In the wake of those troubles, he spent close on three weeks in the city, walking around, talking to people and figuring out ways to solve the problems and rebuild this proud city.

He admits that he was visibly distressed and shocked at the poverty he witnessed during that early trawl around demoralised Toxteth, and that it was

genuine concern. He stresses, though, that his intention wasn't just an exercise to help a ruined and debilitated part of the inner city. "There were vast tracts of Merseyside that were hugely deprived and I felt it was my job to help pull the region out of depression. But my urban policy on Merseyside actually began in 1979, soon after we were elected."

His 13–point 'blueprint' for Merseyside, released in the August of 1981, was considered to be both innovative and wide–reaching: more aid for the young jobless; a massive facelift for run–down council housing estates; an initial £1 million for sporting groups; workshops to be set up in old schools; a boost for industrial estates; and full backing for the police and law and order. He was soon dubbed Minister for Merseyside, a sobriquet he still relishes.

Few, therefore, would argue that Michael Heseltine has stamped his mark on Liverpool and was instrumental in many ways in the regeneration of Albert Dock and the waterfront in general. He is also warmly regarded by all sections of the city, even one–time former rivals in the Labour party and left–wing groups that rose to prominence on the back of the city's dire situation a quarter of a century and more ago.

The initiative to form the Merseyside Development Corporation – charged with reviving Liverpool and the wider

region with a then staggering budget of £200 million – was first mooted in 1979 and his plans for the International Garden Festival of 1984 also predated the riots.

"The situation demanded that people stop moaning; they needed to go out and make things happen. I tried to be the catalyst for that. I know the Garden Festival had its critics but it revitalised 600 acres of toxic wasteland. I made that site available and it should have been used properly later for housing and recreational facilities.

"At the time I had a range of jobs to tackle and the idea of regenerating the south docks and Albert Dock was well along the way. I had learned there were plans to knock it down to make way for a car park. I was horrified and I got there just in time."

Forthright as ever, his rhetoric flows as fast as the river Mersey, which he regards with an affection verging on a passion. Indeed, he confesses that he regards the clean–up campaign for the ailing, grossly polluted river, launched in tandem with the urban development agenda, as one of his proudest achievements.

"When I was staying in Liverpool, I recall sitting in my hotel room at the Atlantic Tower after long, exhausting days of protracted tours and negotiations with various bodies and individuals."

Indeed, not everyone rallied to his call and the local politicians who made up the then Merseyside County Council were aggrieved at his perceived interference; convinced they could help save and revive their own patch if only they had the resources and funding. They resented the Development Corporation and believed it had usurped their authority. Lord Heseltine maintains that his interjection was vital and an integral part of a long–term regeneration for the city and region. In fact, the metropolitan counties were abolished in 1986, although by then he was just completing a term as Defence Secretary. The opposition was thus dispersed; his earlier plans, barely hindered, were rolling on with an unstoppable momentum.

Pondering the issues in the late summer of 1981 as dusk fell one evening over a still traumatised Liverpool, Michael Heseltine had another 'eureka' moment. "My room in the hotel overlooked the river. I would be enjoying a glass of wine as I mulled over what we were doing. It was a tough call as I knew the way forward was to convince everyone that this place, this once great city, was not just a bombed–out wreck; that there really was a future, but it meant pulling together. I was often tired after the day's confrontations and deliberations but didn't feel like sleeping

– the adrenalin surge was powerful, as I knew this was make–or–break time.

"I looked out at this incredible river, so well known to mariners and emigrants the world over and such a majestic, moving sight as it rolled seawards. It struck me that here was another malaise that blighted the city and the area. And I thought, sadly: 'What have we done to you? You are the very lifeblood of this city and we have turned you into an open sewer.' I vowed that something must be done. And it became one of the most emotional and interesting aspects of my time in Liverpool."

The next day he called a meeting of his aides and announced a battle plan. "We have got to save this river. We will go out to the tiny streams of Lancashire and Cheshire and we'll clean the Mersey." So, without further ado, he launched the Mersey Basin Campaign – cleaning the river from source to sea. It has been a spectacular success.

"Despite it being a formidable task, I don't recall any hostility from industry and everyone agreed it was a brilliant idea – but it was acknowledged that, of course, it would take a long time. There was a lot of enthusiasm, as it was obvious that if you have clean water all sorts of other things could happen. Today, the river Mersey has changed dramatically and I believe it is one

of the most important ecological and environmental things that we did."

It is many years since he left government, but Michael Heseltine still visits Liverpool and explains: "Well, you can't just throw yourself into a place like Liverpool and not be moved by the experience. I once planted the acorns for a better future and it is wonderful to see them growing into sturdy oaks and flourishing."

He is delighted at the World Heritage inscription endowed by UNESCO, which hails the waterfront as one of the world's great architectural legacies. "It was certainly not a maritime treasure when we moved in. Now the

Albert Dock is a symbolic achievement of my links to this city and I am so pleased that its heritage is being maintained."

This message was endorsed when, in spring 2008, he was invited to deliver a talk in Liverpool's gloriously restored St George's Hall. Entitled *Liverpool – Reflections and Changes* the talk was part of the distinguished Roscoe Lectures, a series of high–profile events initiated by Liverpool John Moores University and fellow peer Lord Alton.

"Liverpool is certainly on the way back up, although I think there is still a lot to do. I have to confess, though, that I can never forget this city; a part of my heart is here."

'What have we done to you? You are the very lifeblood of this city and we have turned you into an open sewer'

The Mersey is an unpredictable river and can turn suddenly quite ferocious, whipped up by winds in from the Irish Sea and fast moving tides.

# Commanding the Western Approaches

**FRED O'BRIEN**
*Director, Northern Design Unit*

IT is still largely unknown – and certainly barely acknowledged – that during World War II the most important maritime operational site in Britain was located in the basement of an office block in Liverpool.

Here, beneath Exchange Buildings in Rumford Street, the Western Approaches Area Command Headquarters planned and directed the operation of the whole Allied sea and air war. It was the world's first combined operations centre and prototype for all subsequent similar sites.

This command comprised the greatest volumes of ships, personnel and material ever assembled under a single flag. Its operational area extended to 12 million square miles of sea. From below the equator north to the Arctic Circle and from the Mediterranean west to Newfoundland, if an Allied unit flew, steamed or dived, it was known to and commanded from Western Approaches in Liverpool. So extensive and complex

were operations that the command had six subsidiary ports elsewhere in England and Northern Ireland, each with its own admiral.

A high proportion of Royal Navy (RN) and Royal Air Force (RAF) personnel staffing the HQ were female. Women of the Women's Royal Naval Service and the Women's Royal Air Force – known universally as Wrens and Waafs – served there in numerous categories of war work.

All Royal Navy escorted convoys of British and Allied merchant vessels to Murmansk and elsewhere in northern Russia were managed and commanded from this location. It was also the site of the world's first anti–submarine warfare school, attended by officers ranging from Lieutenant Philip Mountbatten – later, of course, to become Prince Philip, Duke of Edinburgh – to admirals for instruction in warfare tactics devised by specialists such as 'No 1 U–boat killer' Plymouth–born Captain Frederic 'Johnnie' Walker.

This tumultuous period is the only time when British and American surface and air units co–operated under unified British command; unprecedented and soon ruled unconstitutional under US law.

The HQ was the epicentre of an intelligence–gathering network extending to north, central and south America, Scandinavia, Europe, the near East and north Africa.

The first commander–in–chief of Western Approaches was Admiral Percy

Noble, who had been in command in Plymouth before the war began. That site had quickly become untenable because of incessant bombardment and hence its relocation to Liverpool.

Noble was a career submariner: tough, decisive and autocratic. He, Johnnie Walker and others devised anti–submarine tactics still in use today.

Early in November 1942 Noble was succeeded by Sir Max Kennedy Horton.

In addition to the RN and RAF the other element vital to victory was the Merchant Navy. Its role and performance was crucial, as without the food and other vital war supplies brought from the US warfare on any front would have been unsustainable. But it paid a high price, losing 3,500 merchant ships and thousands of civilian seafarers.

Liverpool and its people also paid a high price. Four thousand civilians died in aerial bombardments when many thousands of buildings were destroyed and damaged. The people soldiered on; Liverpool as a front–line city showed its toughness and resilience, as it has done through many adversities.

It is worth noting that from mid–1942 Royal Canadian Navy ships, operating mainly out of Londonderry and Belfast, performed half of all merchant convoy escort duties. The British, American and Canadian air units involved were stationed at sites in Merseyside and Ulster.

Until 1960, the Western Approaches

HQ remained a Royal Naval 'outpost' of Plymouth Command, but through the 1970s and 1980s the National Coal Board Pension Fund owned the basement site and the 400,000 square foot building. In 1988 a Liverpool–based development company acquired it but plans for major restoration came to nothing.

On 28th May 1993, the then owner re–opened the HQ as, supposedly, a tourist attraction. The opening ceremony was attended by representatives of 12 navies from countries that had fought the Battle of the Atlantic; the guests included the Russian ambassador to Britain, Boris Pankin, in company with Admiral Ustimenko, commander–in–chief of Russia's northern fleet.

Since then, the so–called museum has opened four days a week between March and October. But there has never been any ongoing Royal Navy or other 'service' involvement, nor association with the Imperial War Museum or National Trust. Sad.

Little, if anything, has ever been done to manifest the crucial and historic importance of this site and less has been done to honour the service and sacrifice of countless servicemen and women.

Western Approaches is below ground – hidden from view – but it is surely unthinkable that it stays buried, ignored and mostly unknown to history, particularly considering its proximity to Liverpool's waterfront and its part in the city's maritime heritage.

*It is a fond farewell as HMS Ark Royal, the main flagship of today's active Royal Navy fleet, sets course for the open sea after visiting Liverpool in June 2008 for the first time in her 23-year history.*

*Sailing dinghies navigate the Mersey during the Wirral Show in July 2008. The show is the largest outdoor event in the UK and is organised by the Wallasey Lions, Rotary and Round Table in partnership with Wirral Borough Council.*

# The Importance of Cotton to Liverpool

**NICK EARLAM**
*Chairman & Managing Director*
*Plexus Cotton*

THE historical importance of the cotton trade to Liverpool, and indeed its huge impact on the city and the world in general, is something I do reflect on now and then from our offices overlooking the Mersey, where we continue to deal in the commodity that helped create the great wealth and reputation of the city.

At the beginning of the 1800s most of the 17,000 or so bales of cotton imported into Britain came through the port of Liverpool and, although cotton is no longer imported into the UK, Liverpool remains at the very centre of the cotton business. Today, about 60% of the world's cotton is traded under the rules established in Liverpool in the 19th century and regulated by the International Cotton Association – until 2004 known worldwide as the Liverpool Cotton Association.

In those early days business was undertaken on the quaysides, in coffee houses or on the streets of the city. Even when a proper base was opened, in 1808, and traders had their offices in New Exchange Building, deals were still largely carried out in the open air, on what became known as Exchange Flags, an area behind the Town Hall.

Our company, Plexus, has been in operation since 1990, when I set up the firm and opened a small office in the former Martin's Bank. Herbert J Rose designed this lovely building and it is now protected through a Grade II listing with English Heritage. It has significant sculptural decorations that refer to Africa's contribution to Liverpool's early economic prosperity and social history.

When we started there were just four of us and I took a great gamble after spending most of my career with the well–known, traditional cotton firm of Meredith Jones. Hard work, an empathy with our partners and an element of luck have paid off and we are now, I suppose, one of the world's leading suppliers of raw cotton, handling in excess of 1.4 million bales of cotton and with a turnover of over US$500 million a year.

We moved to new offices in Birkenhead in 2001, from where we direct worldwide operations that now employ over 2,500 people in locations as far flung as China, India, Africa and South America. The bulk of our clients are actually in the Far East, the Indian sub–continent and Turkey and we source more than 50% of the cotton from Africa. We are, I believe, investing in the long–term stability of the communities where we operate by bringing trade and not just aid.

Liverpool and its waterfront have always been a vital part of both my life and my career, long before I went into the cotton trade as a young man. My father was a director of the legendary Liverpool–based shipping line Elder Dempster, established in 1852 by two Scotsmen. It was instrumental in shaping the important trade between the west coast of Africa and Liverpool.

The fascinating story of this famous line, only wound up finally in 2000, was told in a book – *The Trade Makers* – written by Peter Davies, then Emeritus Professor in the University of Liverpool's School of History.

So, I grew up with shipping, the sea and the river Mersey in my blood, and although I was raised partly in Liverpool and Wirral, I was actually born in Ghana as my father travelled the world with the company. In fact, the family links to the maritime industry go even further back as my grandfather was a doctor in Mossley Hill, conducting his practice amidst the grand and elegant houses owned by rich merchants in south Liverpool. I was told he used to treat 'the great and the good' of shipping magnates such as the Holts.

My own career began as a teenager with Meredith Jones, who dealt in coffee, timber and, of course, cotton. I worked through every department and, at 21, was despatched to the United States for three years to look after the company's interests there.

I eventually came back to the UK and by then was busy buying and selling cotton on an everyday basis, and I figured I could do this equally as well with my own company. So, we sold our house to raise the capital. Traditionally the great cotton traders were family–run affairs but we chose the Plexus name because it sounded modern and reflected our age.

I have a great affection for Liverpool and its maritime history, and we remained for about 10 years in the Martin's Bank building before finding a base in Birkenhead that ironically gives me one of the finest views of the Liverpool waterfront.

*A busy river scene with the overhead cranes at Royal Seaforth Dock standing sentinel over the heartland of the Port of Liverpool's operations.*

*The tug* Canada *carries on its maritime way sailing past the breakwaters built to protect the sandy shore at New Brighton.*

# Chapter 3

*North Docks to Pier Head*

*The World Clipper Race finished in Liverpool in 2008 and pictured is the Durban passing Norfolk Line's Irish Sea ferry vessel Dublin Viking.*

In the foreground lies the wreckage from the original passenger terminal site by Princes Dock with the now redundant Victoria Tower in Salisbury Dock, which still stands proud, while in the background the port continues its daily toil.

*Jesse Hartley was renowned for his Albert Dock masterpiece but he also built 16 other docks and at Salisbury Dock the Victoria Tower boasts a unique six–faced clock with a bell that used to signal high tide and ring out other warnings.*

# Connections Over and Under the River

### Neil Scales OBE

*Chief Executive and Director General of Merseytravel*

THE river Mersey seems to blend effortlessly into the background; to some a simple but stunning backdrop to a city in renaissance, to others the lifeblood of the region over centuries. A hub of commerce and activity for generations, the river has been – and continues to be – a vital way of connecting people and connecting commerce. The same can be said of the region's transport system.

Seamless, integrated transport that makes these connections is vital to the re–birth of the region. It is meshing together people, businesses and leisure activities like at no other time in history, and supporting Liverpool through a period of stunning growth.

Every year around 200 million passenger journeys are made across Merseyside on the various forms of transport coordinated by Merseytravel.

Liverpool, Wirral, St Helens, Knowsley and Sefton. We also own and operate Mersey Ferries and Mersey Tunnels and have a recognised track record as one of the country's best passenger transport authorities.

We work in tandem with public and private sector organisations to support the region's 'excellent' Local Transport Plan and I believe we lead the way nationally through our groundbreaking work to make public transport more accessible.

Under our stewardship, I am proud to say that Merseyrail Electrics is consistently one of the best performing rail networks in the country, while the Mersey ferries are the number one paid-for tourist attraction in the region. And the Mersey tunnels are the safest tunnels in the UK with Queensway – the older of the two – the safest tunnel for its age in the whole of Europe.

We were one of the official partners in Liverpool's Capital of Culture year in 2008 and I am convinced that it provided a further catalyst to the region's transformation, supporting economic growth, regeneration and the region's booming tourism sector.

This is most visible in our investment in the world-famous Mersey ferries: a fixture on the waters of the Mersey for more than 800 years. Indeed, Benedictine monks at Birkenhead Priory founded the first ferries in 1150AD, charging a small fare to row passengers across the river.

In 1318 Edward II allowed the Priory to provide board and lodgings for travellers waiting to cross the river,

a matter of days or weeks during the worst weather. In 1330 his son, Edward III, confirmed the Royal Charter to operate the ferry. It is translated to read: *"That they and their successors for ever might have the passage over the said arm of the sea, as well as for man as for horses as for other things whatsoever and may receive for the passage what is reasonable without let or hindrance."*

This made the Birkenhead to Liverpool ferry a royal highway, still marked to this day by the crown on the gangway posts at Woodside and the Pier Head. In 1538, Henry VIII began the dissolution of the monasteries in England and the ferry rights were granted to Sir Ralph Worsley. They have since changed hands a number of times throughout the years.

During World War I, the ferries *Iris* and *Daffodil* were commandeered to act as additional troop carriers for a raid on U-boat pens in Zeebrugge, in April 1918. They had large carrying capacities, double hulls and shallow drafts for sailing over minefields, and they were able to navigate the shallow waters close to the target – the Mole. The object of the raid – which was a huge success – was to neutralise the German U-boat operations threatening Allied shipping, particularly in the English Channel.

Both ferries survived and the battered flotilla limped home to a heroes' welcome. King George V decreed that because of their exploits the vessels – and their successors – should be given the titles *Royal Iris* and *Royal Daffodil*, and they are still in use today.

The ferries came under

Merseytravel's control in 1968 following the passing of the Transport Act. We re-launched them as a significant visitor attraction in 1990, investing millions of pounds in the refurbishment of the ferries, including the *Royal Iris*, *Royal Daffodil* and *Snowdrop*. Indeed, investment since 1998 alone has been around £50 million.

And the ferries have been totally repositioned to become the region's most popular paid-for tourist attraction, as well as a convenient and colourful way to cross the Mersey. Ferry services now include commuter journeys, daily River Explorer cruises and other special cruises, including trips along the Manchester Ship Canal; they are also available for hire.

We have also invested in our three ferry terminals: at the Pier Head on the Liverpool side of the river and at Seacombe and Woodside in Wirral. And we are delighted at the success of the stunning space-themed attraction, Spaceport, which opened in 2005 at Seacombe. It has hosted two hugely successful *Doctor Who* exhibitions, amongst other events, and the terminal is also home to Play Planet, a café and a kart track for children.

We were conscious for a long time that the ferry terminal at the Pier Head needed radical changes and so we demolished the old building. The £10.5 million terminal that replaced it – which is very much in keeping with the waterfront's World Heritage site status – offers hugely improved facilities for passengers, commuters and the hundreds of thousands of visitors using

the ferries every year: retail outlets, café, waiting areas and a Beatles-themed exhibition.

Of course, we were aware of the impact that the building might have on its surroundings and the low-rise design was specifically chosen so as not to impose on the spectacular view of the 'Three Graces' from the river and the views of the river from Water Street and Brunswick Street.

We also decided to extend the existing Beatles Story at the Albert Dock into the terminal. It incorporates a magical four-dimensional theatrical journey through the music of the Beatles complete with motion, smoke, water and smells.

However, one of my favourite projects is the installation, at the Woodside ferry terminal, of the German submarine *U-534* as an intriguing and interactive exhibition and tourist attraction. The submarine was rusting away, its fate uncertain, on Wallasey docks for several years after the closure of the Historic Warships collection in 2006.

The 1,200-tonne boat – believed to be one of only four left – was launched in February 1942 and was one of the last U-boats to be sunk by the Allies in 1945, just two days before the end of the war in Europe. She was never involved in active combat but carried out vital meteorological operations as well as being used for training.

On 5 May 1945 *U-534* was sailing in Kattegat, north-west of Helsingor, and ordered to surrender, but refused. She was attacked, taking heavy damage, although 49 of the crew of 52 survived. She was raised in 1993 and landed up in Birkenhead as part of the warship collection.

It is a story that fascinates me and I have done considerable research into its background; I even have a two–metre long model of the boat in my office. On its journey from Wallasey to Woodside, transported by the floating crane Mammoth, we had to cut the boat into five sections, using diamond–studded wire.

Apart from running the region's train network, buses and ferries, another of our key activities involves operating the two Mersey tunnels – Queensway and Kingsway – through which around 80,000 vehicles cross under the river every day.

The 'grand old lady' is Queensway, which is a single–bore, 3.24–kilometre, two–way tunnel that was opened by King George V on 18 July 1934. It cost £8 million to construct over eight years and eight months and was ranked financially as the biggest single municipal enterprise ever undertaken in the UK. Work started on Kingsway in 1966 and was opened by Queen Elizabeth II in June 1971. It is almost 2.4 kilometres long and consists of twin tubes.

In 2006 we launched a series of sightseeing Tunnels Tours, which tell the history and inner workings of the tunnels, with a behind–the–scenes look at their operations. They also take in a visit to the escape refuges deep under the river and allow unique access to the engineering control room. Visitors can also see one of the six giant ventilation fans in action.

In June 2008, as part of our commitment to European Capital of Culture, we held an historic 'Under and Over the Mersey' event, when more than 12,000 people of all ages enjoyed a rare chance to walk through a closed tunnel and then travel back across the water on a ferry. It was only the fourth closure in the tunnels' history for a walkthrough.

Another of our exciting programmes is the investment in public artworks at key gateways to Liverpool. These include a statue of comedian Ken Dodd linked with the late political firebrand Bessie Braddock, located at Lime Street station. It features the work of renowned Liverpool sculptor Tom Murphy and is, I believe, one of the jewels in our public artwork collection.

And we haven't overlooked the waterfront, which is one of our major showcases in many ways. An installation commemorating the life of John Newton by sculptor Steve Broadbent – a former student of the legendary Liverpool sculptor Arthur Dooley – provides a visually amazing backdrop for the Pier Head ferry terminal.

To some, the river is part of the region's history: the foundation on which this great city was built. To others, it has the potential to be just as much a part of our present and our future.

'The ferries have been totally repositioned to become the region's most popular paid–for tourist attraction, as well as a convenient and colourful way to cross the Mersey'

*The clipper Jamaica arrives in Liverpool at the end of the World Clipper O8 race.*

*The Waterloo Docks – now Grade II listed – were built by George Fosbery Lyster as a grain store in 1867 and the quaysides were the scenes of large–scale migrations to America. The building was refurbished in the early 1990s to provide luxury apartments.*

*Taken from Everton Brow, a fabulous sun sets over a tranquil Liverpool while in the background, across Wirral, can be seen the rolling Welsh hills.*

# Defining Liverpool's Identity

**JIM GILL**
*Chief Executive, Liverpool Vision*

WHEN the first cruise liner passengers stepped ashore at Liverpool's Pier Head in September 2007 they became a symbol of Liverpool's renaissance, attracted once again to an international outward–looking city with a name that resonates across the globe.

If the cruise ships are coming, courtesy of a new terminal for the 21st century, then you know things are happening in Liverpool, because the waterfront is integral to the identity and experience of the city. Their voyage brings them to a city engaged in its own voyage of transformation and they disembark onto a World Heritage site that is at once a monument to Liverpool's glittering past and a vision of the city's future.

The Liverpool story is directly linked with the ebb and flow of waterfront activity. The waterfront that we have helped create is an attractive visitor–focused environment with improved pedestrian and public transport links to the wider city centre and, clearly, the world beyond. Now, once again, the city's waterfront is playing a full and vital role in the city's ambition, status and destiny.

Liverpool owes its very existence to its geography and its access to the sea. Eight hundred years ago it was little more than a community of fishermen. But by the end of the 19th century it had been transformed into the greatest port on earth. Liverpool's international prestige was reflected in the majesty of the 'Three Graces' at the Pier Head.

During the course of the 20th century, at first slowly, then more dramatically, Liverpool's fortunes changed for the worse. The influence of the sea and seafarers on the city had waned. Liverpool's Atlantic advantage, so important in its growth, now made the port unsuitable to capitalise on the new trade with Europe. The advent of containerisation saw the port activity creep further and further northwards. Gradually, Liverpool turned its back on its most important physical attribute. By the 1970s the most striking image was of derelict Albert Dock warehouses surrounded by silted–up docks.

The refurbishment of the Albert Dock in the 1980s was one of the main achievements of the Merseyside Development Corporation and its private sector partner Arrowcroft: but that development didn't have the hoped for catalytic effect. For over 20 years this magnificent building complex stood in splendid isolation, disconnected from the core of the city centre and without supporting development to encourage people to stay by the river.

But the city was changing and the waterfront was a key element in that change. Driving our vision were a series of ambitious and exciting landmark projects that would establish the waterfront both as a place to be enjoyed by Liverpool's citizens and as an international visitor destination.

The landmark project is the Arena & Convention Centre at Kings Waterfront. It is providing a massive boost to the city's economy and has injected a new lease of life into the Albert Dock.

Across the Strand, the retail–led Liverpool One development has shifted the city's centre of gravity closer to the waterfront. Together with the attractions at Kings Waterfront, Albert Dock and Mann Island, it provides a compelling draw for visitors to the city.

Liverpool was once regarded as the second city of the Empire precisely because it exploited its natural advantages. Our challenge was to recapture and exploit these advantages with a major programme of new developments, interventions and connections, while respecting the historical and architectural context reflected in World Heritage site designation.

The prize of a successful Liverpool waterfront is huge. It places the city firmly back on the map of world cities and creates opportunities for the people of the city through employment and leisure activities in a way that even the port in its heyday failed to do.

The Mersey waterfront remains the key attraction for outside interest. It provides a spectacular gateway to the city, a link with the cultural and historical attractions elsewhere in the city and wider region, and demonstrates to the outside world our new–found confidence.

For me, today's waterfront is an inspirational sight, no longer a vision of desolation on the edge of a tired and backward–looking city. From my office window overlooking the Pier Head I see a daily changing scene, from cruise liners to aircraft carriers, from tall ships to ro–ro vessels, the daily ferry crossings, leisure trips and the 'Steam Packet' boats; along with a sea of hard hats and a festival of cranes building Liverpool's future. And most importantly, a constant stream of people visiting and enjoying the waterfront.

The river Mersey and its waterfront frame and define Liverpool's identity. Our waterfront is iconic, a symbol of Liverpool and not only when times are good. Liverpool has again moved closer to the water's edge, physically and psychologically – an eloquent statement of its current confidence and global ambition.

*A scene showing the symbiotic relationship between the city and the river.*

# Chapter 4

*Pier Head and Three Graces*

*The best vantage point for a splendid view of Liverpool as these two sightseers sitting on a wall close to the Seacombe Ferry Terminal will confirm.*

*The weather comes in dark and brooding giving Liverpool an almost Gothic feel.*

# A Well–loved Landmark the World Over

**Peter Mearns**

*Executive Director, Marketing & Communications*
*The Northwest Regional Development Agency*

WHENEVER I'm asked in an official capacity to comment or reflect on Liverpool's waterfront my response is always clearly defined, stressing that the agency understands the significant economic potential and that we are committed to supporting projects that will help enhance its appeal.

And, although my remit is to cover the whole geographical spread of the North West of England, it is, I feel, important to point out that Liverpool's waterfront is a major gateway to the region. It is an internationally recognised symbol of the city and one of its greatest assets, which is why we've invested millions of pounds in a number of development schemes.

It is a truly unique and inspiring part of the city. Yet, as I'm extolling the virtues of its distinctive architecture, the born in the city, an attachment that I think gives me a deeper perspective on what the waterfront, and indeed the wider Mersey estuary, mean to so many people.

My great grandfather, Joshua Brabbins, was also born in Liverpool and lived and worked in the city for many years before emigrating to Vancouver at the turn of the last century. He plied his trade as a cabinetmaker specialising, so I understand, in billiard tables. Tragically, his first wife and youngest son had died of typhoid and so he went to make a new life for his family in the New World with his daughter and another of his sons.

The family story relates how his eldest son Alfred – my grandfather – remained in Liverpool to complete his engineering apprenticeship at Cammell Laird and never joined his family in Canada as he fell in love with Amelia, my grandmother, and they made a life together in Liverpool.

My mother told me that Joshua went on to marry twice more, once coincidentally to another 'Scouser' living in Vancouver. He worked for the rest of his life in the logging business but would make infrequent visits back home to Liverpool. It seems he travelled overland from Vancouver on the Pacific coast to Canada's east coast, and then on to Liverpool by sea – a formidable return journey in those days of around 12,000 miles.

He would also bring exotic gifts of native woodcarvings. My mother remembers the Albert Dock in Liverpool where he berthed being a hubbub of activity, packed with transatlantic

passengers and, usually, all of Joshua's extended family in the city, who would gather to greet him.

So, when Liverpool was inscribed with UNESCO World Heritage status – based on its position as a maritime mercantile city – it was an accolade I fully endorsed on several levels, particularly as it reflected its significance as a commercial port at the time of Britain's greatest global influence, in the 18th and 19th centuries.

Along with the prestige of European Capital of Culture for 2008, the UNESCO acknowledgement has helped to propel the city back onto a worldwide stage in these early years of the 21st century. It underpins the fact that the area is of immense cultural and historical importance; not only does it confirm Liverpool's rightful place in world history, but it also gives the city a marvellous platform from which to market itself – and the waterfront – as a world–class location to visit, live and invest in.

Tourism is, of course, an essential ingredient of that marketing agenda – as well as a key economic driver – and we, as an agency, were given responsibility for tourism policy across the North West some years ago by central government. We established five tourist boards, all with their distinctive characteristics; all promoting themselves as part of the region but also individually. The majority of our visitors are from across the UK, but we do have a large contingent from north America as well as from the Far East, including China and Japan.

Liverpool is a big draw in Japan because of the Beatles connections and now that the city is twinned with Shanghai it is increasingly a draw for Chinese tourists and trade delegations. I think Liverpool's slogan for its European cultural year – 'World in One City' – was a wonderful term that encapsulated so many things, reflecting contemporary attractions as well as the city's maritime legacy.

The agency was set up in 1999 by the government and its role has changed and developed over the years. Our emphasis now is on providing a strategic leadership for the region and a catalyst for sustainable economic growth. We are also responsible for directly influencing public and private sector investment into the region in support of the regional economic strategy, an economic blueprint for the North West crucial to sustainable economic growth.

It is also our job to improve the perception of the North West – and the region's highly individual locations such as Liverpool – as a place to visit through marketing and promotional programmes.

The regeneration activity on Liverpool's waterfront is undoubtedly one of the highlights of the exciting Mersey Waterfront programme, which involves an exhilarating plan to boost the attractions of the 145 kilometres of coastline that frame part of the wider area, taking in parts of Cheshire, Liverpool and northwards as far as Southport.

The thinking here is to connect the waterfront's wide–reaching

communities and assets across the urban districts of Sefton, Wirral, Liverpool and Halton and so create an internationally acclaimed waterfront configuration that rivals Toronto or Sydney.

Historically Liverpool was a hub for the great passenger liners of previous eras – it was, of course, the home of Cunard for decades – and we were convinced that we could once again attract some of the world's great cruise ships to the river Mersey on a regular basis.

Therefore, we committed £10 million to help bring this idea to fruition, aware of the significant increase in visitors that could be generated by the cruise industry, never mind raising Liverpool's profile as a major international cruise destination. That investment went towards the £19 million landing stage that enables the giant cruise liners of today to mark Liverpool on their maps.

And our support for – and investment in – the award–winning Arena & Convention Centre on the banks of the Mersey helped to create what is readily recognised as a striking addition to the riverfront. From our strategic agenda we believe it boosts the local economy by more than £100 million and its distinctive design quite rightly won the prestigious Royal Institute of British Architects' award for what was called "a significant contribution to the historic river frontage of the Mersey".

It is a strong and recognisable symbol of the lasting legacy that European Capital of Culture leaves for Liverpool and we are proud to have played a part in that project.

Furthermore, our commitment to the Museum of Liverpool – with a £32 million package – helped to kickstart the regeneration of the whole of Mann Island at the Pier Head. We believe that this world–class facility, housed in a striking contemporary building, is very much in keeping with the nature of World Heritage sites. Without a doubt in years to come it will be hailed as one of the world's leading city history museums, reflecting Liverpool's global significance through its unusual geography, history and culture and thereby encouraging tourism to the city and the North West region.

Liverpool's waterfront has inevitably changed over the centuries and its contemporary evolution continues that tradition. The most dynamic of those innovations in the last 50 years or so is the extension of the Leeds and Liverpool canal. It runs alongside the waterfront, across the Pier Head, in front of the Three Graces, and into the south docks complex. We were so convinced of the benefits that we invested £7 million in this British Waterways–run project to create a vibrant water space that provides a fascinating new focal point for the Pier Head.

I'm sure that my great grandfather, Joshua Brabbins, wouldn't recognise the physical layout of Liverpool's waterfront today, but I think he would agree that the hustle, bustle and sense of vibrancy that marked it out in his time has continued. The waterfront was and still is a remarkable landmark, known and loved the world over.

'Liverpool's slogan for its European cultural year – 'World in One City' – was a wonderful term that encapsulated so many things, reflecting contemporary attractions as well as the city's maritime legacy'

*A warm sunny glow taken in the early 1990s before the riverfront was dramatically changed in style and substance by new buildings.*

*The 'grand old dame' of the sea QE2 arrives in Liverpool for the first time in July 1990 when more than one million people turned out to see her.*

# A Lifelong Watery Love Affair

**PETER GRANT**
*Journalist, poet, cartoonist & book editor*

HAND in hand at the Pier Head. "You know the river Mersey," I said. "It's like the river Danube. If it looks blue – then you are in love. Does it look blue to you?" She threw a stone that rippled across the water endlessly. She turned, shrugged, and said: "No, it looks absolutely murky to me."

I wrote that when I was 11 – forever the romantic. I reckon it will always look blue to me. I grew up in the Vauxhall area of Liverpool 3, the only one of five brothers born at home. Paul Street was not too far for my dad John 'Gunner' Grant to ride his bike, called 'Iron Horse', to the many Liverpool docks he worked on before and after World War II. A docker, and proud of it.

He would tell me of exotic places – such as the Princes, the Belfast and Waterloo docks.

I recall going down to the waterfront with mum to pass him sandwiches and meeting his mates, all wearing caps and smiles on faces etched with kindness.

Tough men, yet men all sparkling with a down–to–earth warmth I have never forgotten.

Some would take off their oily gloves and dip into pockets to give me a coin and pat me on the head. They were giants in more ways than one to such a little lad, awestruck by a busy world in the early 1960s.

And they all had a quaint Liverpool aroma – salt water mixed with something I later found out you could only get in pubs. The *Liverpool Echo* would be sticking out of their bags. They were a living community, where laughter was as common as ships' horns.

Years later I would draw boats of every description in art classes at school and it instilled in me a love of everything maritime. My parents told me that everyone loved the waterfront and, at weekends, people would flock to the Pier Head in their smart clothes to chat, meet up and maybe go down to a tavern in the town for a sing–along.

I recall being a self–appointed midshipman at the age of 12 on the ferry to New Brighton and seeing the magnificent buildings sail out of view: the Liver Building, Custom House and the Port of Liverpool Building. I loved playing on the sands and in the fun fairs, but I wanted to be back over there ... home. Now, half a century old, I understand and appreciate the river, the city's lifeblood, which is part of my make–up.

For a number of years I was fortunate to work for *Port News*, the

paper published by the Mersey Docks & Harbour Company – our office was in the imposing Port of Liverpool Building at the Pier Head. During that time I met the generations of dockers and port workers who had inherited a twinkle in their eyes from proud fathers and grandfathers.

I have painted the Liverpool World Heritage skyline for friends. Many of those watercolours of the 'Three Graces' now grace the walls of homes in Australia, America and Canada.

Granted it's a city full of problems, but it has learnt from past errors. Now it is born again, with – as the famous song says – a realistic hope in its heart.

When I have worked away from the city I've missed it so much. In Birmingham I was told that one day the Brummie city would have the finest inland waterways for tourism. "It has more canals than Venice," I was told. I responded, in my Scouse accent, that I was pleased, but "Birmingham isn't Venice".

The Liverpool waterfront is world class. It still inspires writers and singers, the likes of Willy Russell and Roger McGough, whose dad was a Seaforth docker. John Lennon actually wanted to sail on the *QE2* and slip back into his home town. But his dream was over ... taken out of his hands. John used to sit and look out into New York bay and tell Yoko how much it reminded him of home. At the end of his bed was a sea chest stamped with the word 'Liverpool'.

The waterfront for John and the rest of the Beatles was a source of inspiration. Any photograph of this image cannot fail to move those born in the city and those who no longer live here but continue to feel part of it. I still write poems now, just like that 11–year–old lad looking up at the seagulls and smiling at what lay ahead out there.

Hand in hand at the Pier Head. "You know the river Mersey," I said. "If it looks blue then you are in love ..." Well, we split up the next day. The girl and me, not me and the river Mersey.

Oh no, I still love her; and she looks every bit as blue as when we first met.

*Nightfall and the lights of the waterfront lend an air of magic to the Pier Head.*

The famous Liverpool club Cream brought its cult Creamfields Festival to the city's waterfront to welcome in the 21st century at New Year 2000.

# Celebrating the Liverpool Waterfront

Professor John Belchem

*Pro–Vice Chancellor, University of Liverpool*

ANNIVERSARIES, it would seem, are good for Liverpool, a city renowned for firework displays and street celebration. By happy coincidence, such festivities have tended to occur at times of prosperity and optimism, high points in the city's roller–coaster modern history.

The 700th anniversary, in 1907, of the granting of letters patent in 1207 proudly displayed the 'second city of Empire' in full Edwardian glory, at the very acme of maritime and commercial prosperity. Fifty years later, the 750th anniversary was celebrated with futuristic fervour, heralding an end to inter–war depression and post–war austerity through the belated advent of industrial diversification. However, just as the port–based economy before it, the new industrial 'boom town' was soon to collapse, along with the vibrant 'Merseybeat' it helped to foster. The 'shock city' of post–industrial Britain, much maligned Liverpool managed to and creative enterprise. This time, it is to be hoped, the optimism and economic promise will be sustained.

There are grounds for hope. Once the last fireworks of 2008 are forgotten Liverpool will retain what will surely prove its prize asset in the lucrative market for cultural tourism; its status as a UNESCO World Heritage site. True to Liverpool's past as a great port city, the aptly named Liverpool Maritime Mercantile City World Heritage site extends beyond the waterfront into the urban heart. It embraces the 'commercial centre' around Castle Street, Dale Street and Old Hall Street, now increasingly residential and 'desirable' as commercial palaces are transformed into luxury apartments, restaurants and wine bars; the William Brown Street 'cultural quarter', where Victorian civic pride in 'Liverpolis' reached its zenith, a heritage preserved with requisite commercial 'visitor attraction' acumen by National Museums Liverpool; and the warehouses and merchants' houses of Lower Duke Street, historic buildings which contribute much to the character of the 'Rope Walks', the parallel narrow streets which now provide the main focus of the city's thriving night life and creative industries sector. However, it is the remarkable waterfront that occupies pride of place.

Extending in either direction beyond the Pier Head, the World Heritage site runs from the Albert Dock conservation area, already one of the leading visitor attractions in the North West of England, through to the Stanley Dock conservation area, where the sheer scale but pinched interior construction of the gargantuan Tobacco Warehouse, closed since 1980, all but defy any re–use or regeneration. At the centre lies the Pier Head, a remarkable early example of urban recycling. With commercial space at a premium in opulent Edwardian Liverpool, land was reclaimed from a redundant dock to provide the ground for a stunning transformation of the built environment. The domed Mersey Docks & Harbour Building was completed – with a due sense of history and celebration – in the jubilee year of 1907; the skyscraper Royal Liver Building was finished in 1911, its clock set in motion at the precise moment that the crown was placed on the head of the new monarch, but the intended name 'Great George' was not to take hold; and then, finally, the Italian renaissance palazzo of the Cunard Building opened in 1913 – just before World War I took its toll on Liverpool's fortunes – to complete the iconic and photogenic sea–facing 'Three Graces' skyline by which Liverpool remains instantly recognisable.

In many ways, the Pier Head forms an appropriate epicentre for the World Heritage site. Facing out to sea and with its back turned on England, it symbolises for many the fabled Liverpudlian spirit of independence and proverbial sense of apartness. Its cityscape appearance suggests an affinity with developments across the Atlantic, also evident in the port city's precocious cosmopolitan profile, propensity for 'machine' party politics and prowess in popular music – there are also, of course, strong visual echoes on the Shanghai waterfront. Above all, the very site of the Pier Head, on land reclaimed from the Mersey, is a reminder that Liverpool's history is best understood in terms of human geography.

Written at the time when the Pier Head was being reclaimed, Ramsay Muir's *History of Liverpool*, specially commissioned to mark the 700th anniversary in 1907, concentrated on the interaction of physical location and human endeavour. For centuries after its establishment as a planned town on a greenfield site in 1207, the 'borough' of Liverpool barely developed beyond a largely agricultural and fishing village and had few attributes to distinguish it from a rural settlement. Insignificant, obscure and out of the way, Liverpool eventually made its presence felt through remarkable investment in a transport infrastructure of turnpikes and canals: here were the beginnings of an effective transport infrastructure for the developing economic region of south Lancashire, Cheshire and north Staffordshire, facilitating an internal triangular trade carrying such vital commodities as salt and coal. There was also the construction of the first commercial wet dock – now buried beneath the Liverpool One shopping development.

Driven by a combination of mercantile ambition and civic power, the Council in the early 18th century drew upon the security of the Corporation estate to fund this risky, speculative but spectacularly successful enterprise.

Having tamed the Mersey's 30–foot tidal range, commercial Liverpool exploited its hard won comparative advantage, establishing itself as the western emporium of Albion. With a proactive – and comparatively youthful – risk–taking mercantile oligarchy at the helm, unrestricted by chartered companies or medieval guilds, Liverpool's remarkable history had truly begun. Boosted by the slave trade – the horrors of the external triangular trade were by no means minimised by Muir – modern Liverpool underwent exponential growth to become one of the world's greatest ports, a human "miracle of transformation" quite without rival, symbolised by a massive dock system "as solid and enduring as the Pyramids, the most stupendous work of its kind that the will and power of man has ever created".

This pioneer form of what we would probably now call public–private partnership set a pattern in Liverpool, providing the means for the city to reposition itself and redefine its economic rationale. A century or so later, in the midst of inter–war depression and the collapse of world trade, the city's move into industry was facilitated by another set of major transport infrastructure projects, such as the Mersey Tunnel and the East Lancashire Road and – a further example of visionary civic enterprise – the pioneering Liverpool Corporation Act of 1936 which established industrial estates in Aintree, Kirkby and Speke. As yet, however, there has been nothing on a similar public–private scale to aid the latest rebranding exercise around creative and cultural activities. In its present–day inflexion, partnership government has yet to deliver on prestigious strategic priorities.

The lack of a *'grand projet'* notwithstanding – whether a 'fourth Grace', some other world–class signature building or merely a reintroduced tram system – the regeneration has proceeded apace. Behind the waterfront, the transformation of the city centre has been a considerable achievement, although not without critics. Liverpool, they fear, is following the pattern of Glasgow, the last British city to enjoy European city of culture status, in 1990: a rapidly regenerating and gentrifying urban core surrounded by a ring of intensely disadvantaged residential areas. Others have questioned the sustainability of the city centre boom itself given Liverpool's continuing 'relative deprivation', although the statistics they cite lag somewhat behind the cranes and the developers, the latest dating back to 2001, when the average household income throughout Liverpool was just 79 per cent of the national figure. Perhaps this is why Harvey Nichols have yet to consider Liverpool a suitable site for their upmarket operations in the north – significantly, Harrods dropped their plans for a Liverpool store in 1920 as the brief post–war boom came to an end, a symbolic precursor of the city's downward spiral in the inter–war decades. As well as being dated, these figures fail to take account of the high levels of disposable income of visitors attracted to the city, whether Euro–rich

Dubliners visiting their weekend second apartments in Liverpool, a staggering reversal of former migrant flows, or affluent 'cultural' tourists whose ever–increasing numbers are fuelling a hotel boom.

Amidst the concerns about redevelopment, the World Heritage site points the way forward through a policy of regeneration through conservation – appropriately the most significant new build adjacent to the Pier Head is the Museum of Liverpool. So far the kind of 'sailortown kitsch' noted by my colleague Graeme Milne in fashionable waterfront urban renewal elsewhere has been avoided. Outside its boundaries redevelopment is more problematic. While much improved in appearance, the city centre is beginning to look like any other city centre. Must regeneration be at the cost of Liverpool's distinct identity, that edginess and otherness so cherished in its past? Fortunately, there are some examples of best practice, not least on the precinct of my own university, where the new administrative building provides a successful post–modern juxtaposition with the Victorian Gothic splendour directly across Brownlow Hill. Now reflected in the steel and glass of the Foundation Building, Alfred Waterhouse's magnificent Victoria Building, the original 'redbrick', has been transformed into the Victoria Gallery and Museum to house the university's art and heritage collections. The only such new facility to open in Capital of Culture year, the Victoria Gallery and Museum serves as a reminder of Liverpool's

remarkable architectural heritage – it is an unfortunate irony that Waterhouse, son of a local cotton–broker, is best known not for his native Liverpool buildings but for his great work in Manchester and London. By restoring the building to its former glory, and putting it to new use, the university has rejuvenated the knowledge quarter in the best Liverpudlian tradition. Through understanding its past and recycling its use, Liverpool can be confident of its future.

'True to Liverpool's past as a great port city, the aptly named Liverpool Maritime Mercantile City World Heritage site extends beyond the waterfront into the urban heart'

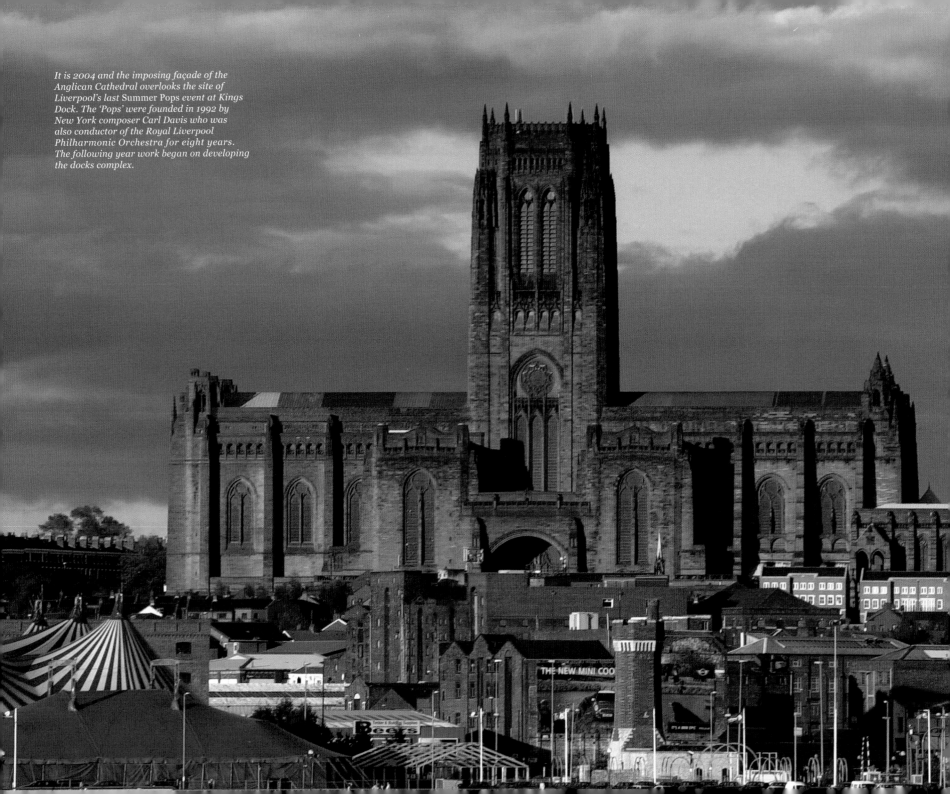

*It is 2004 and the imposing façade of the Anglican Cathedral overlooks the site of Liverpool's last Summer Pops event at Kings Dock. The 'Pops' were founded in 1992 by New York composer Carl Davis who was also conductor of the Royal Liverpool Philharmonic Orchestra for eight years. The following year work began on developing the docks complex.*

*A rainbow lights up an area of the waterfront, perhaps heralding a 'golden' period of change for Liverpool, that was to be kick–startd with the building of the 134–metre Beetham Tower that was completed in 2004.*

*A view of Liverpool from the promenade along from the Woodside Ferry Terminal.*

*The moon rises over Liverpool on Boxing Day 2004 just before Liverpool begins to really kick–start its regeneration programme in 2005.*

# Liver Fortress Standing Sentinel

Steve Burnett

*Chief Executive, Royal Liver Group*

AS tall as 22 double–decker buses stacked on top of one another, two massive towers, four gargantuan clock faces and a pair of iconic birds; that is the Royal Liver Building. It is a mighty site, the largest of the magnificent 'Three Graces' at Liverpool's Pier Head.

It is also a somewhat imposing sight; at least it is to those that see it for the first time – this enormous granite fortress that stands sentinel over the city. And that is just what it is, a fortress built to protect people.

At Royal Liver we have spent 158 years protecting people – since we were founded as the Liverpool Lyver Burial Society by nine local working men in the Lyver Inn on July 24, 1850.

Our founders believed that they could make a difference to people's lives by helping them find peace in death ethos still remains; we are here solely for the benefit of our members.

Perhaps that is why the people of Liverpool do not see our towering waterfront headquarters as imposing in the same way that I did when I first visited the city as a boy in the 1990s, which proved to be the catalyst for my move from the South East.

Having now spent some years here, I think that the people of Liverpool see the Royal Liver Building – like the waterfront itself – as a great source of pride. They link it with their own identity, as a symbol of a strong heritage that has survived the years, always changing and re–inventing itself whilst remaining true to its principles.

Our Liver Birds have seen many of Liverpool's changing faces over the years – through both good and bad fortune – from the decline of the docks and the war years to the 'swinging 60s' and, perhaps more exciting still, the renaissance that began in the 1980s with the Merseyside Development Corporation and which has played a major part in the city's status as European Capital of Culture in 2008.

When I moved here, in 1996, I quickly saw Liverpool as a city with a great heart and soul – a vibrancy and zest for life.

I have always seen the waterfront as that heart – beating now for more than 800 years – with the people as the soul and the river the lifeblood.

My personal perspective allows me to be a part of Liverpool's beating heart every day and, as I make my way to the office, I am captivated afresh by the 'Three Graces', the warehouses, the docks and the new developments.

I think of Royal Liver as a microcosm of Liverpool. We have a strong identity, a lot of history, most of our staff are local but a good number are from outside of the city and we are building for the future. It is this mix of personality, heritage, local pride, cosmopolitanism and forward planning that makes Royal Liver what we are – the people give us our soul, just as they do Liverpool itself.

A World Heritage site, Liverpool's waterfront is one of the best known and most striking in the world. The 'Three Graces' are the highlight of that vista and, completely without bias, I think that the Royal Liver Building is the jewel in their crown.

I have been told by some staff, with great pride, that we are the only one of the 'Three Graces' to be Grade I listed – probably because we are one of the earliest examples in the world of the pioneering technique that allowed the construction of such a radical building.

I have also been told by other staff, with great relish, that we were the architectural inspiration for New York's Manhattan Municipal Building and the Seven Sisters in Moscow.

Our clock, the Great George, is a source of satisfaction too. Larger than the dials of Big Ben, its huge faces put wry smiles on the faces of Scousers.

Then there are the Liver Birds, the icons that perch proudly on our two towers. Undoubtedly the most famous elements of the Royal Liver Building – and of Liverpool's waterfront – they are recognised the world over.

The myth goes that if the Liver Birds fly away Liverpool will sink into the Mersey; that is how much they mean to the people here. They are no longer just Royal Liver's birds. We are now the custodians, but they belong to everyone in the city in the same way as Royal Liver, a mutual organisation, is owned by every one of our members.

The powerful image of the Liver Bird as a cultural icon in Liverpool, indeed, some might say a symbol of Liverpool itself, probably stems from the city's maritime heritage. For generations, the last images of their home that sailors leaving Liverpool would see were the towers of the Royal Liver Building, with the river–facing Liver Bird watching over them and guiding them to their destinations as they made for the open sea. That same Liver Bird has also welcomed back generations of sailors returning to the city – their first sight of home after a long voyage.

Then there is the Liver Bird which looks out over the city, standing guard over the people of Liverpool, keeping them safe and providing inspiration, just as it has done on numerous occasions since it first perched on the east tower.

Like when World War I broke out in 1914 and we announced that we would give extra support to members affected by the Great War, a move that was to become legislation shortly afterwards.

There was also 1920, when the 'great wave of unemployment' saw many members fall into arrears but, rather than cancelling their cover, we changed our rules so that members could maintain their policies. Further economic crises came from 1926 and on into the 1930s, with a miners' strike, the General Strike and the Great Depression; again, we suspended forfeiture notices.

Then, during World War II, we found ourselves in the thick of the action when the Royal Liver Building became *HMS Eaglet*, part of the Admiralty's North Atlantic operations masterminding vital naval escorts for the merchant ships crossing the U–boat infested Atlantic.

In addition, the chapel housed in our basement allowed servicemen and women to attend services or spend a few moments in private prayer without having to leave their station. The basement also served as a hospital for wounded sailors as they returned to port.

Liverpool is a city where community, values and pride are the traits of everyone. That is why, when I look at the waterfront – the ever–changing waterfront – with the signs of prosperity, growth and hope all around, I think I might just feel the same sense of awe and the same sense of pride as felt by a native Liverpudlian.

I see Royal Liver's history, our ethos, our values and our plans for the future as a microcosm of the city. For me, the waterfront sums up all of the city's hopes, ambitions and values.

Royal Liver's history is inextricably linked to that of Liverpool itself; both growing from humble origins – a local pub and a small fishing village – and changing since Victoria's England to emerge into the 21st century with renewed pride and vigour.

It was fitting that during Liverpool's year as European Capital of Culture we celebrated the 100th anniversary of the laying of the Royal Liver Building's foundation stone.

We also celebrated 2008 by working with our nearest neighbours in the Chinatown and waterfront communities on a number of projects. They are now as much a part of Liverpool's waterfront as the new developments, docks, warehouses and grand commercial buildings and we will continue to work with local people to promote culture, regeneration and community.

It is flattering that the Royal Liver Building has come to be known as one of the 'Three Graces'. In mythology, the 'Graces' are not only beautiful, they also represent peace and hope.

I am sure our two neighbours at the Cunard and Port of Liverpool Buildings would agree that this is something that Liverpool's waterfront has always done well, and will continue to do well on into the future.

'For generations, the
last images of their home that sailors
leaving Liverpool would see were
the towers of the Royal Liver Building,
with the river–facing Liver Bird watching
over them and guiding them to their
destinations as they made for
the  open sea'

*The cityscape takes on a different form than that so familiar to earlier generations of sailors as the classical old buildings merge with their 21st century neighbours – viewed from Bidston Docks in Wirral.*

# Sic Transit Gloria Mersey

**Andrew Harrison**
*Associate Editor of* The Word

TO those raised in the Merseyside sprawl the Liverpool waterfront is both the ends of the earth and the beginning of the outside world. Gazing out from the Pier Head you feel you are standing on the very lip of reality; the Irish Sea winds cut through you on their way up to Lime Street but also stir possibilities in the mind. The mysteries of Dublin or the clamour of New York seem only a few steps away.

The grey expanse of plaza between the Liver Building, the Cunard Building and the Port of Liverpool Building is an open–air departure lounge which gives rise to thoughts like these. It may be no more than a trip to Seacombe on the *Royal Daffodil* today, but tomorrow you could be going anywhere. For good and ill, Liverpool has always been an international city. To stand on the Pier Head and feel winds from God knows where, to see beyond the Bar to God knows what, is to feel yourself a citizen of the world.

The Pier Head is Liverpool's face and its armour, a living logo in stone and reinforced concrete that tells you where you are and what you can expect. Here it is in the title sequences of *The Liver Birds* and *Brookside*, framing all that we're about to see. There it is, blurred by a downpour and crazily tilted, on the cover of Frankie Goes To Hollywood's troubled second album *Liverpool*, as if to say that all you can do when you've experienced the sybaritic delights of the Pleasure Dome is to fly home as fast as you can. Even when Liverpool's waterfront profile is invisible, it's still there. Here's Ian McNabb, former 'Icicle Worker' hymning the city's indestructible womenfolk in distinctly nautical terms: 'She's a Liverpool girl, don't wear a coat, the laughter from her golden throat can be heard from the Irish boat... my Liverpool girl'.

As a teenager I wanted to be a journalist and I would work the summers in the environs of the Pier Head for a news agency called City Press. From an office in the Port of Liverpool Building, my older mentors would enunciate stories down the phone to the punctilious copytakers of the *Sunday Mirror* and the *Sunday Times* because faxes had not yet been invented, never mind email. I would make the tea, report on dockers' darts tournaments for the Dock Company's *Port News*, which we produced amongst other publications, and sometimes I would help with headlines. When roll–on roll–off freight services went 24–hour at Liverpool Freeport, we ran with 'WAKE ME UP BEFORE YOU RO–RO', which remains a source of pride to me to this day. After months of pestering, I finally got to review the odd band for the *Daily Post* and then the *Liverpool Echo*.

The City Press office was beneath one of the famed domes or 'drums' on the corners of the Port Building – still my favourite of the three majestic structures that give the Pier Head its identity. The building is beautiful from the outside, a mighty Baroque statement of permanence and solidity which slowly grew ironic as the port became neither permanent nor solid by the 1980s. Within, though, it was a maritime temple: a circular atrium under a giant dome, scale models of the great ships in glass cases all around you, the points of the compass in marble beneath your feet and, above you, circling the hall in gilt, the words of Psalm 107 explaining the building and explaining the city: *'They that go down to the sea in ships – that do business in great waters – these see the works of the Lord and his wonders of the deep. Anno Domini MCMVII.'* I never tired of walking into the Port Building on a blazing hot day. It smelled of history – and other things.

Once, the staff of City Press decided to effect entry to the giant glass–windowed dome above our office on the north–west corner of the Port Building to discover what was inside. Navigation charts from the heyday of trade on the river? Disused communications equipment for the Western Approaches Command of World War II, when Liverpool was the Allied lifeline? When we opened the door, an avalanche of dead pigeons filled our office and we had to go to the pub to recover. *Sic transit gloria* Mersey.

Those were the days of Militant, and from the roof of the Port Building we saw parts of Liverpool's municipal drama played out at the Pier Head. There was the much-reported anti-Militant demonstration, a strange affair in which a silent majority, clearly unfamiliar with this protest lark, turned out to register their disapproval of the city council's collision course with the government - golfing umbrellas were seen.

Years later I lived in New York and found in Manhattan's monolithic architecture strange echoes of the Pier Head. The detail on the Cunard Building, it turned out, was inspired by the American *beaux–arts* style. The Manhattan Municipal Building at the bottom of Broadway is basically an overgrown Liver Building topped by a gilded lady named 'Civic Fame' instead of the Liver Birds – not much of an improvement, really. Then I married a New Yorker, Lily, and when I showed her the Liverpool waterfront, she felt at home too. Standing on the Pier Head, the world feels only a zone ticket away.

*Early in 2003 construction work starts on Liverpool city centre and the waterfront.*

# The Balance Between Commerce and Culture

## Professor Phil Redmond CBE

*Chairman of National Museums Liverpool
and Chairman of The International Centre for Digital Content (ICDC),
and founder of Mersey Television*

LIVERPOOL is an old city with a relatively recent past. On its 800–year timeline things did not really get going until the final quarter. But when they did they became one of history's ripping yarns. From sleepy fishing port to global mercantile centre; second city of Empire; the industrialisation and then abolition of slavery; one of the world's first mega–cities; at one time arguably the most vibrant city on earth; and, then, to the brink of bankruptcy.

Staring into the abyss of obscurity the city has stepped back and begun a renaissance based not on the bricks and mortar or sandstone and cobbles of the past, nor even on the steel and glass of more recent times, but on its greatest resource: its people, their shared lifestyle, their shared culture.

To understand this, as in all great

vision. A city whose commercial profits funded philanthropic culture. A city that turned to its cultural heritage to survive its commercial downturn. A city, the rise, fall and renaissance of which can be encapsulated in three chapters: commerce not culture – commerce and culture – commerce from culture.

Built on the banks of the river Mersey Liverpool, like most port cities and like the tides that ebb and flow around them has for most of its history been at the centre of nothing yet on the periphery of everything. A city on the edge; a city swept along, or blown aside, by global rather than local winds. This inevitably leads to a resident population serving transient needs and growing to distrust the status quo and those who espouse it.

This is why central governments, of all hues, have often had difficulty engaging with the local population. It is not just a British phenomenon but can be seen across the world as port cities struggle with centrally driven policies that ebb and flow like the tides, too often pedalled by what are perceived as transient carpetbaggers. Whether right or reasoned is of no matter, it is a fact and characteristic of the local psyche. Ignore it and you will struggle; embrace it and you will prosper. It's based upon respect. Give respect for the city's – and therefore the people's – timeline, and you will receive it in return.

With 2007 seeing Liverpool's 800th anniversary that timeline must begin in 1207 with the granting by King John, not of a charter but Letters Patent, bestowing the right to develop the

township as a mercantile centre based roughly on a grid of six streets. It was perhaps the city's first large–scale property development and those six streets exist to this day, a short walk from the largest property development in the city's history; the Liverpool One shopping district. This in itself brings a touch of historical continuity, perhaps even irony to the story, as Europe's largest retail development is funded by Grosvenor Estates under the patronage of His Grace the Duke of Westminster. In a city famed for its labour movement *noblesse oblige* has a continuing role in this story.

Still, despite the royal intervention of 1207 nothing much seemed to happen in the following 500 years. Chapter one seems to start in the early years of the 18th century as at the end of the 17th century Daniel Defoe was already marvelling at the way Liverpool had tripled in size. Around the same time, in 1695, a real Royal Charter was granted, ending control by local landed interest, and the story picked up pace. A city council was formed, although far from anything we would recognise as democratically accountable.

Comprised of local merchants who shared a common vested interest in the development of the port, commerce and associated trades, there is no doubt that today they would be rounded up and charged under various anti–competitive and consumer protection legislation. Naturally, though, things seemed to get done. And quickly.

The world's first wet dock was commenced in 1707, starting a 200–year

expansion that led the port to become the second city of Empire and gateway to the world, with over 10 miles of docks along both sides of the Mersey. By the time London opened its first dock in 1802, Liverpool already had over 2.5 miles of dock quayside and as the industrial revolution, and our story, began to pick up speed a new dock was added approximately every six months. This 19th century docks building programme was largely engineered and built by one man, Jesse Hartley, working to a Docks & Harbour Board that was also nothing more than a committee of the council. Obviously, never a health and safety officer or hi–visibility jacket in sight.

And here, in our risk averse age, the storyteller finds another interesting twist in the historical tale: the lack of formal qualifications or experience amongst the central characters in the city's growth and cultural heritage. Hartley was one, as were George Stephenson, William Roscoe and Henry Tate; all connected by a cultural convergence revolving around the time, place and what is probably Hartley's greatest legacy, the Albert Dock, the world's first fully enclosed dock. Surrounded by warehouses to provide a wind–free environment for the square–riggers the Albert Dock is now regarded as one of the world's great buildings, a model for ports around the world including St Katherine's Dock in London and Buenos Aires' Puerto Madero Dock.

Thus, Hartley remains a central character, not only in Liverpool's story but also, arguably, one of the greatest

influences on the developing industrial age. Without Hartley's skill in dock design and engineering Liverpool's role as the gateway to the world might have been hindered and, consequently, the flow of trade, people and ideas that swept through his dock gates and across the globe. Yet, when he took on the job of dock surveyor he had no experience of dock construction. He learned the trade, as it were, on the job. Of course, this was not a barrier to career development in the early 19th century. Just a few miles away, around the same time, a virtually illiterate railway engineer called George Stephenson was laying the first tracks in the world's first intercity link – between Liverpool and Manchester – thus sparking a revolution of global impact. Railways spread across the globe but, by linking what became known as the crucible of the world, the coal, iron and steel of the North West, Stephenson's railway lines joined Liverpool's shipping lines to allow the import and export of goods to a level never before seen, and all flowing through Hartley's developing docks system.

If chapter one closed with these two early practitioners of work experience plying their trade and building their careers, chapter two was already underway by 1831 when William Roscoe was coming to the end of his life. Roscoe had left school at the age of 12, apparently because he felt he had learned everything his school teacher could teach him. He later self–educated to become a successful lawyer, but takes his place in history as the 'founder of Liverpool's culture'; using his own wealth and encouraging others to establish museums, galleries, libraries, academies and botanical collections. It was Roscoe, the anti–slavery campaigner, who took the city into its second stage: chapter two – commerce and culture.

Without Roscoe to persuade, usually by example, commerce to fund culture, Hartley's memorial of the Albert Dock would not now be housing the Liverpool Maritime Museum, the International Slavery Museum and Tate Liverpool. The latter gives us our final link to this interesting confluence of commerce and culture. Tate founder, Henry Tate, was born in 1819 and educated at a school his minister father ran for the 'education of the poor', but by the age of 13 he was apprenticed to his older brother in a Liverpool grocery shop.

Twenty–six years later, at the height of a boom time for Hartley's docks and Stephenson's railway–building, the poorly educated Tate had eight shops in and around Liverpool and was on his way to establishing the great Tate & Lyle sugar refining empire, the profits from which would fund the collections for and establishment of the Tate galleries.

Looking back almost 100 years those central characters, perhaps unknown to each other, created a format out of which Liverpool's story and character evolved: people and their ideas, unhampered by the status quo and pushing in new directions whilst embracing new thinking and new technology.

For a city like Liverpool, always distrustful of the status quo and waiting for the next wind of change, the adoption of new technology holds no fears. Just as the networks of docks and railways created the wealth to fund the transition from commerce to culture, then so too may the modern networks of telecommunications and the internet offer similar opportunities.

Already there are signs. The Beatles, the Mersey Sound era, writers, poets, artistes and footballing fame all came on the back of television in the 1960s and later the media explosion of the 1980s. Today, the still developing internet beckons, heralding global winds of change over the next 10 years as connection speeds and capacity increase – a quantum shift, like going from Stephenson's *Rocket* to Nasa's space shuttle.

History shows us that when technology allows a greater volume of trade and knowledge transfer the citizens of Liverpool are not slow on the uptake but, like all good stories, the audience should be left wanting more.

That is Liverpool. And the story is not yet finished. Two of the three chapters have been written. Only time will dictate what comes next. Perhaps another storyteller, looking back at the city's millennium in 2207, will add the next chapter? Perhaps someone will dig out a copy of this book and validate the idea that the city grew through three ages: commerce not culture – commerce and culture – commerce from culture.

'Liverpool, like most port cities and like the tides that ebb and flow around them, has for most of its history been at the centre of nothing yet on the periphery of everything. A city on the edge; a city swept along, or blown aside, by global rather than local winds'

*Ferry 'Cross the Mersey... another journey across the river made famous in the song by Gerry Marsden,*

*Mooring bollards at the Cammell Laird shipyard on Wirral add a nautical flavour to the classical view of the Liverpool waterfront; a photograph taken in 2003, only a year before 'regeneration and redevelopment' were to start transforming the face of the river frontage.*

*The tugs of the Mersey are the traditional 'work and shire horses' of the sea...*

*Sunset over Liverpool as it prepares to wake
to a new dawn...*

*It is May 2008 and the 20,000 tonne ms Astor cruise vessel visits Liverpool.*

# The Long and Winding Road to Recovery

Jack Stopforth

*Chief Executive, Liverpool Chamber of Commerce*

AT the risk of sounding glib, the regeneration of a city is a journey, not a destination. It has no starting point and is never completed, even when key milestones beloved of planners and economists – full employment, increased GDP per capita, desirable levels of skills in the workforce etc – are passed. In the last 100 years, Liverpool's journey has been rockier than most – from Edwardian eminence, to national whipping boy during the 1970s and '80s, to European Capital of Culture and model of regeneration in 2008.

Liverpool's reputation and self–image, like its politics and economics, have been shaped by larger–than–life characters as diverse as William Gladstone and Derek Hatton; Sir Simon Rattle and John Lennon; Samuel Cunard and Sir John Moores; Dixie Dean and Bill Shankly; or Shirley Valentine and Yozzer Hughes. This is, self–consciously, a cauldron of popular culture, high art, supply lines between Britain and North America. The city was bombed relentlessly and saw much of its housing and public infrastructure destroyed. And yet Liverpool briefly regained something of its pre–Depression prosperity under the wartime economy and Liverpool Corporation's policy of building out–of–town industrial estates for the munitions industries would provide a foundation for a new industrial future into the 1950s and beyond. The 'homes fit for heroes' central planning mentality of the Attlee government favoured interventionism and that was essential for reconstruction.

But after the War ended many of Merseyside's fundamental problems remained. Wartime bombing had added to decay in exacerbating a severe housing problem. Returnees and rapid population growth were too much for a faltering labour market and the Port of Liverpool lost ground to competitors in the south and south–east. The impact of these changes was not confined to dock workers but also damaged the professional heart of the city – shipping services, ships' chandlery, freight forwarding, marine insurance, commodity trading, distribution services, transportation and literally dozens of ancillary activities.

Liverpool's economy was over dependent on trade links with the Empire that would become less important in the new European and North American dominated world order. But for the granting of Development Area Status in 1949, these problems would have seemed even more

formidable. As it was, remarkably good progress was made during the '50s.

In the early 1960s, the premiership of Harold Wilson, MP for Huyton, was instrumental in creating a substantial motor vehicle manufacturing cluster in Merseyside and thousands of new jobs were generated by Ford, General Motors (Vauxhall), Standard Triumph and their suppliers. The arrival of these modern industries shielded Liverpool against mass unemployment in the early and middle years of the decade and the city enjoyed a short–lived boom. The '60s was an optimistic decade, with Liverpool and Everton FCs dominating the football world and, of course, the Beatles putting Liverpool at the epicentre of the 'Swinging Sixties'.

However, the new jobs were only a temporary relief and the seeds of political and economic trouble were already evident. Nationally, the ports and shipbuilding industries were decasualised at the cost of thousands of traditional port jobs. By the time Barbara Castle published her White Paper *In Place of Strife* in 1969, the inherent culture clash between the disciplines required by the new manufacturing sector and Liverpool's tradition of casual employment led inevitably to workplace conflict. It was in this period that the city's damaging reputation for poor labour relations emerged.

Macroeconomics and geopolitical change made things much worse. In 1967 the Wilson government devalued the pound; the base lending rate rose to eight per cent and, as conflict in

the Middle East sent fuel and raw material prices soaring, inflation climbed. Membership of the Common Market in 1973 gave a further turn of the screw, as customers of the Port of Liverpool lost the benefits of 'Imperial Preference' and the Mersey docks had to compete with smaller and cheaper ports on the east coast.

The sugar industry represented a microcosm of the city's plight. Massive sugar cane refineries owned by Tate & Lyle simply could not be adapted to process European sugar beet instead of West Indian and Australian cane and were decommissioned in the late 1970s and early '80s. Along with the refineries went an entire industry employing several thousand people. Dedicated shipping lines, docks and warehousing facilities were suddenly redundant; the once commonplace blue–and–gold liveried Tate & Lyle tankers were mothballed and the superstructure of sugar buying, trading, shipping, insuring, refining and distributing was rendered obsolete.

The docks shed thousands of labourers as the changing technology of shipping meant bigger vessels, greater mechanisation, fewer bulk cargoes and increased containerisation. The bigger tankers and container vessels needed deepwater berths and mechanical handling that could not be accommodated in the oldest parts of the dock system, south of the city centre. Consequently, the focus of port activity moved north towards Seaforth.

Liverpool's dock estate, incorporating both sides of the river

Mersey, comprised 11 linear miles of docks – easily the biggest in the world. The restoration of these Victorian docks and warehouses would later prove hugely significant, but when they closed they represented nothing but obsolescence. Other industries too were changing radically. In the late 1970s and much of the '80s my colleagues in the county council coined the phrase "Friday night is closure night" as dozens of manufacturing and processing businesses shut down and even the motor industry was not immune, as the closure of British Leyland's TR7 sports car factory showed. Unemployment exceeded 20%.

The industrial troubles of the 1970s were socially corrosive and discontent was crudely politicised in the '80s. A reactionary central government provoked an equal and opposite reaction in local government. The Militant Tendency exploited the position for its own pseudo–revolutionary aims. Unemployment in Merseyside was around 20% when Toxteth exploded, along with similar inner city communities in Bristol and Brixton. But only Liverpool was demonised and romanticised in equal measure, depending on whether you watched television programmes such as *Panorama* or *Boys From the Blackstuff*.

Despite – or perhaps because of – this political and social unrest we saw in the 1980s the start of the recovery the city region is at present enjoying. Merseyside County Council did important work on key roads and infrastructure and created the

Merseyside Enterprise Board. The Mersey Docks & Harbour Company secured the Liverpool Freeport and the county council and newly formed Merseyside Development Corporation (MDC) jointly kick–started the revival of Albert Dock by developing the Merseyside Maritime Museum. The momentum was sustained by the MDC when they went into partnership with private developer, Arrowcroft, to restore the rest of Albert Dock.

The whole process was dogged by the running ideological battles between Liverpool City Council and central government. This bruising clash made Michael Heseltine's personal intercession, post–Toxteth riots, all the more remarkable. Heseltine was Secretary of State for the Environment in a government at loggerheads with a Militant city council and yet he became Liverpool's unlikely advocate in government. As the self–styled 'Minister for Merseyside' – and subsequently – Michael Heseltine's contribution to Liverpool's recovery cannot be overstated.

The obvious public manifestation of his work was the International Garden Festival, opened by Her Majesty the Queen in 1984, but in reality his influence in securing investment from the City of London and advocating public expenditure in the inner cities was far more significant. Indeed, in the mid–1980s, when he had moved on to become Defence Secretary, his support for the struggling shipyard of Cammell Laird led directly to an order to build the

Type 42 Destroyer, *HMS Sheffield*, keeping the yard going for years.

The abolition of the Merseyside County Council in 1986 had created a vacuum, with the power struggle between the city and districts not helping economic growth; but the latter part of the decade saw a crucially important development. Far–sighted officers of Liverpool City Council, notably deputy chief executive, Alan Chape, realised that if the area's GDP per capita fell below 75% of the EU average then Merseyside might qualify for Objective One funding.

Some of the more hysterical press equated Liverpool's economy with Italy's Mezzagiorno, or the poorest regions of Greece. In fact, those southern European areas had a GDP as low as 25% of EU averages while Liverpool's was fractionally below the 75% trigger point. Even so, European funding was as crucial to the 1990s and the early years of the 21st century as Development Area status had been to 1949.

The process of investing massive Objective One resources in a comparatively small area over a relatively short timescale has had dramatic results, leading to a return of confidence and investment. The same formula was the key to one of the most successful City Challenge programmes in the UK (1992–97). Liverpool City Challenge was a considerable success in mobilising the city's development community and property scene.

Another critically important contributor was – and is – higher education. Liverpool University and,

especially, Liverpool John Moores University were extraordinary catalysts for property development.

However, we will only be genuinely self–sustaining when our private sector is as big as the public sector. That is still some way off, but closer than it has been for decades.

'In the last 100 years, Liverpool's journey has been rockier than most – from Edwardian eminence, to national whipping boy during the 1970s and '80s, to European Capital of Culture and model of regeneration in 2008'

*It could be Venice... but it's the main dome of the Port of Liverpool Building competing with the heavenly style of the Anglican Cathedral.*

*The* Grand Princess *dwarfs the Liverpool
waterfront in August 2008 – summer a
mere wish as lowering skies lend the scene a
brooding almost threatening atmosphere.*

*The QE2 berthed at the Pier Head at the cruise liner terminal several hundred metres from Cunard's old headquarters just past the Liver Buildings on the right.*

# Why the *QE2* Stirs the Emotions

**TONY STOREY**
*Journalist and Writer*

IT takes something of style, splendour and size to overshadow Liverpool's 'Three Graces' and it doesn't happen often. The first time I can recall the focal point of the city's waterfront shifting was on a brilliant summer's day in 1990 – Tuesday, 24 July to be precise.

That was 150 years, give or take a week or two, after Sir Samuel Cunard's paddle steamer *Britannia* had left the Mersey bound for Halifax, Nova Scotia and Boston. Cunard's historic crossing of the north Atlantic took twelve and a half days and marked the dawn of an age of transatlantic travel by ships bearing his name which continues to this day.

To mark its 150th birthday, Cunard Line despatched its then flagship *Queen Elizabeth 2* on a celebratory lap around the British Isles, with the call at Liverpool billed as a likely highlight. Some highlight. From the moment the mighty Cunarder dropped anchor mid–Mersey, just off the Pier Head,

until she left almost 16 hours later under the glow of a spectacular firework display, the 'Three Graces' were indeed overshadowed.

Her first call at Cunard Line's spiritual home had attracted more than a million people to the banks of the Mersey, providing a timely reminder of the pulling power possessed by the region's greatest natural asset. That day, and well into the evening, it was as if each and every one of those one million spectators had some connection with the river or the port or the great liners that had plied the ocean routes before *QE2*.

I was working at the *Liverpool Echo* at the time, where we'd planned an ambitious day's production of special editions to mark the historic inaugural call by *QE2*. As the day unfolded, thousands of words crossed the sub–editors' desks and hundreds of images landed with the picture editor.

Only when we had chosen those to fill our editions, and the last one had gone to press, could I stroll round to the waterfront from Old Hall Street to see what all this excitement was about. *QE2* at anchor in the Mersey that day was an amazing sight – the sort to make a strong impression on those witnessing such a spectacle for the first time, or to stir the deepest of memories and emotions among those more familiar with the sight of Cunarders in the river Mersey.

Since that first memorable call *QE2* has returned a further seven times to the

Mersey, capturing the imagination of hundreds of thousands of onlookers over the years.

During one of her arrivals, in July 2000, I stood on the bridge as we passed Crosby beach at dawn. To the naked eye the sand looked black. Through binoculars, it was actually thousands of people lining the shore to welcome the return of the most famous ocean liner in the world. Half an hour or so later I caught the first Mersey ferry alongside *QE2* at anchor and strolled from the Pier Head to the office. Not a bad way to make the journey to work!

Her last visit to Liverpool marked the opening of the city's long–awaited cruise liner terminal – the landing stage which once again allows the floating palaces of the age to tie up at one of the most famous waterfronts in the world.

That night, floodlit and tied up alongside at Liverpool for the first time, *QE2* struck her most lasting impression on the Mersey waterfront. People in their thousands thronged the Pier Head and Princes Parade. Late in the evening was more like teatime rush hour along the Strand.

There was a buzz about the place that night. *QE2* berthing within sight of the Cunard Building helped to put the city's unique maritime heritage into a sharper focus.

Ships have since come and gone at the berth, some big and some small, but none attracts the crowds quite like *QE2*.

She makes history and breaks records pretty well everywhere she goes.

She was built at the John Brown shipyard on the Clyde in Scotland and was known only as 'Job number 736' until she was officially launched by the Queen in September 1967 – and she was the last passenger ship to be built on the Clyde. In 1982, she was requisitioned by the government for service in the Falklands Campaign – and so joined the ranks of the great 'Cunarders' called upon to serve the country in times of conflict.

She is, though, not actually named after the Queen. Her full name indicates instead that she is the second ship to have been called the Queen Elizabeth. The famous liner is 963ft long, 105ft wide and can carry as many as 1,778 passengers and more than 1,000 crew – and has a top speed of over 32 knots.

Now after sailing almost six million nautical miles, crossing the north Atlantic 806 times and carrying a total of 2.5 million passengers, retirement has beckoned for *QE2*. She will not pass our way again. But none who saw her on the Liverpool waterfront will ever forget the experience.

*The prow of the proud QE2 slips gently past the Pier Head waterfront heading for the open seas during a visit in May 2004.*

# The Splendour of Wirral's Waterfront

. Steve Maddox OBE

*Chief Executive, Wirral Borough Council*

SO many of the world's greatest cities are focused on waterfronts that are truly awesome: inspirational locations such as Cape Town, Santiago, Singapore or, indeed, Liverpool, our nearest neighbour, with its memorable and globally renowned waterfront.

Yet, in the endless struggle for regeneration and visitor attractions, the paradox for Wirral's own extended Mersey waterfront is that its banks allow the grandest, most panoramic views of Liverpool's splendid river frontage of architectural gems, including the 'Three Graces'.

This was underlined during the visits of the Tall Ships to the river, in 1984, 1992 and the summer of 2008. There was only one place where everyone wanted to watch the parades of sail – from Wirral's own waterfront on the waned, and now wax once again in the early part of the 21st century; that great maritime city basking in a modern–day prosperity linked to a positive attitude towards the challenges of a new era.

On our side of the Mersey, it was Cammell Laird and Lever Brothers that were the prime movers in Wirral's industrial heritage and port–related activities that formed the mainstay of the local economy. International links also established Birkenhead as an important shipping centre and the docks continue to play a vital role in Wirral's economy, where today new enterprise flourishes and businesses prosper in this 'peninsula of opportunity'.

Industrial and commercial entrepreneurs have always found Wirral a convenient and suitable location and, while we can reflect on the once mighty Cammell Laird shipyard, the contemporary revival of the Birkenhead docklands areas at Twelve Quays by the Port of Liverpool, now a part of the Peel Holdings transport and property group, is an indication of how the future will pan out; while the Norse Merchant Ferries who ply their trade between Ireland and Britain are an important transport and maritime hub for the region.

There are those who might – in a kind of disparaging way – refer to Wirral as Liverpool's 'dormitory', but we are inclined not to take umbrage at this, as we are aware that about 40% of the people who live in Wirral work outside the borough – most of them in Liverpool. So they have the best of both worlds: they work in the city and choose to live here, where they can also get the best view of Liverpool.

And, in any case, we have our own proud historical legacy to dwell upon. Once an area of scattered villages and hamlets, engaged in farming and fishing, Wirral is actually mentioned in the Domesday Book and by other ancient chroniclers.

The focus of our agenda is to regenerate the waterfront on this side of the Mersey. We want more people to come and live on the peninsula. Part of our task is to raise the profile of Wirral both in the UK and internationally – to show off the excellence that we have here in real estate, views and quality of life.

We wish to change the face of the Wirral waterfront – to bring in fresh ideas from outside, rather than just looking from within – and to put a focus on international connections. In fact, Wirral's tourism strategy identifies the waterfront and large stretches of coastline as our greatest asset, which clearly is underpinned by Peel Holdings' long–term development plans, including the Wirral Waters scheme, probably one of the most exciting concepts I've had across my desk.

In my view, wide stretches of docks and hinterland are a hugely valuable asset, much like Shanghai's Pudong was to that city in the 1990s – and look how that has been transformed in just a decade or so.

More than 300,000 people live here and we are, of course, not a city, although we try to describe ourselves in those terms. Historically we are made up of five different townships – including Birkenhead and Wallasey – that, since 1974, have had a kind of corporate identity, and which we are now trying to promote as a region. In effect, I suppose we are a 'municipal area' – a municipality – and I think this is our great strength.

A fascinating historical note is that Wirral boasts only the second official American Civil War heritage site outside of America, as recognised by the White House–sponsored Civil War Preservation Trust: the other place is Cherbourg.

And the Confederate warship *CSS Alabama* – a ship that became infamous for its role as a blockade buster against Union navy forces – was built in No4 Dry Dock at Cammell Laird in Birkenhead. Indeed, it is common knowledge that many Liverpool and Wirral cotton merchants, and others dealing in a more perfidious trade, were supporters of the Confederacy, despite the official British government stance of the time.

In fact, the last formal surrender of the American Civil War (1861-1865) took place aboard the *CSS Shenandoah* in the river Mersey, just off Tranmere, some six months after the hostilities ended.

The sprawling docks complex around Twelve Quays and the Birkenhead waterfront has always been symbiotic with Liverpool, as have the ferry links that act as umbilical cords, joining both sides of the river, as do the underwater tunnels that allow both motorised vehicles and trains to connect the two separate geographical entities and mingle the populations.

But, although often in the shadow of its more high–profile neighbour, Wirral has an individuality and diversity that bestow on it a level of enlightenment, emboldened by a feisty spirit. It has a clearly focused perspective of its own identity, forged by a natural environment of outstanding beauty – surrounded as it is by water on three sides – surely the key to Wirral's distinctive character and moods.

So, whilst we may be on opposite sides of the river, Wirral and Liverpool share a cultural and industrial background and heritage that forever bind us together – and, hopefully, futures which overlap.

*Fishermen near the lock entrance to Birkenhead docks just down from the Seacombe Ferry Terminal take advantage of the vastly cleaned up river Mersey.*

*The summer of 2008 and the river bustles with craft of all shapes, sizes and origins – making a super sight is the Mexican navy's sail training ship* Cuauhtmoc.

# Connecting People With the River

**JUDITH FEATHER**
*Mersey River Festival organiser*

WHEN I joined Liverpool City Council, way back in 1975, I had no idea that my new career would be so exhilarating, interesting and rewarding. As it has turned out my life's work over the following 25 years would involve organising hugely diverse programmes of sport, maritime, cultural and civic events, some of the largest staged by any city in the UK.

One of the most challenging periods spanned 2007 and 2008 as these years, respectively, saw the celebration of Liverpool's 800th birthday and Liverpool's year as European Capital of Culture.

Liverpool's events programme has always been dynamic and varied and each year there have been new events to organise, whether the commemoration of the 50th anniversary of the Battle of the Atlantic or Olympic boxing.

It was in late 1995 that Liverpool City Council was asked by the soon–to–be–abolished Merseyside Development Corporation to take responsibility for the funding and delivery of the annual Mersey River Festival.

This event, begun in 1981 under the auspices of Merseyside County Council, had been the catalyst for the visits in 1984 and 1992 of the Tall Ships' Races to the river Mersey.

The events team had no experience of organising maritime events and, indeed, there was doubt expressed in some quarters that the transfer of the festival to the city council was a good idea. These reservations were soon dispelled.

In fact, in 1991 we staged the first ever '5th November' river Mersey fireworks and music display and this event quickly established itself and saw some 50,000 spectators coming to the waterfront each year.

Over the following eight years my team and I worked tirelessly with river pilots, both retired and active, harbourmasters, the Royal Navy and many other maritime–related organisations, sailing clubs and individuals to stage the festival, which just got bigger and better over subsequent years.

One of the key objectives was to attract visitors to the city but it was also to get Liverpool people to come to the waterfront to watch, participate and to connect firmly with the river. I hope that we managed to achieve that, and certainly the success of the event inspired all of us involved in organising it.

The festival atmosphere was electrifying and the programme featured tall ships, navy ships, sailing ships, film replica ships, racing yachts, steam boats, narrow boats and motor vessels of all shapes and sizes, some famous, some not.

The Mersey International Shanty Festival, maritime street theatre performers, aerobatic displays, a photographic competition, Royal Marine helicopter rescue displays, 'Have a Go' at water sports sessions, regattas on the river and a Parade of Sail all featured in the programme.

Organisations such as the Merseyside Maritime Museum and Merseyside Police all provided additional action packed displays.

The maritime community gave generous support in time and expertise and this united effort created a very special event.

The popularity of the festival provided the catalyst for the city council to agree to sponsor and, subsequently, host the Clipper Round the World Yacht Race, Sea Liverpool 2005 as one of the European Capital of Culture themed years, the Honda Powerboat Grand Prix series and the Liverpool Sail Training Initiative.

During this period the Liverpool waterfront was, of course, also awarded World Heritage status.

The city council also recognised that the time was right for another bid to bring the Tall Ships to the river Mersey.

This, too, was successful and, in 2008, the magnificent Tall Ships' fleet was berthed in Liverpool's historic docks. One million people are estimated to have seen the ships whilst they were at their berths or on the river during the Parade of Sail. In aggregate audience terms this was the biggest event in the Capital of Culture calendar.

The challenges of staging maritime events whilst the waterfront was still being developed in such a major way prompted the city council, with the permission and co–operation of Peel Holdings and United Utilities, to open up part of the Central Docks to the public. Again, thousands flocked to see the 'All Aboard' event, which was in effect a mini Mersey River Festival.

The Mersey has provided a 'stage' for many exciting events and there is a collective determination to continue developing a world–class maritime programme to compare favourably with the best maritime cities the world over.

The cruise liner berth also provides further opportunities for river–based events and the people of the city always give the warmest of welcomes to visiting cruise ships.

The Liverpool waterfront is a very special place – and a unique natural asset – and it has been and is both an honour and a pleasure for those who have had the privilege of staging events on the river and along the waterfront, and who have benefited from the support of the maritime community.

*A Tall Ship scoots between two Royal Naval vessels in the summer of 2008.*

*A firm favourite with Liverpool crowds, HMS Ark Royal was given a warm welcome in June 2008.*

# Reflections on the Two Bunds

**KERRY BROWN**
*Executive Director*
*Liverpool Shanghai Partnership*

THE formal twinning of Liverpool and Shanghai may only date back to 1999, but anyone who has visited the two cities can see a visible demonstration of their historical links in their respective waterfronts.

Nicolas Pevsner, in his monumental survey of the buildings of England, described the 'Three Graces' that look over the Mersey from Liverpool's reclaimed shore – these buildings were all built where marsh once was – as one of the great waterfronts of the world: a suitable place for embarkation, or departure, to new lives. Perhaps he had never been to Shanghai because the Bund, the series of 29 buildings alongside the Huangpu river, matches, echoes, and in many ways stands as a precursor to the architectural statement on the other side of the world in Liverpool.

Looking from the Mersey ferry across to the 'Three Graces' you get a sense of Liverpool's unique, outward–looking past, but also of how, with the new developments along the water's edge both up– and down–river, Liverpool is striving to shape its present and future.

Shanghai too has been engaged in a process of reinvention over the last century. A city built much later than Liverpool – it was only founded in the 1850s – its early history was always associated with the arrival of foreign merchants, diplomats and, in many cases, chancers and daydreamers. By the 1900s, at about the time that Liverpool's 'Three Graces' were being built, the Bund was already well established. The great line of hotels, offices, banks and government buildings that perch along the Huangpu and Suzhou rivers today was the achievement of foreign and Chinese architects, western capital and Chinese labour. As in Liverpool, these mighty buildings were put, inauspiciously, on soggy marshland.

People like to see Liverpool's influence on Shanghai in the Bund buildings, as opposed to the thriving new commercial city of Shanghai on the other side of the river at Pudong. The most magnificent of the Bund buildings, the great Customs House – where even today the bell tolls out Communist China's anthem 'The East is Red' – and the old Hong Kong and Shanghai Bank headquarters next door, each have stylistic similarities with the Royal Liver Building and Customs House in Liverpool. They were roughly contemporaneous. At its time – around 1909 – the Royal Liver Building was the largest steel–supported structure in the world. But direct links are tenuous.

Shanghai's Bund was to have one distinct difference to Liverpool's 'Three Graces'. It was to go through years of war and revolution, and the scars from this tumultuous period are still etched on the faces of many of the buildings today. In 1943, when Chiang Kai–shek, the leader of nationalist China, made Shanghai the battlefront in the war against the Japanese, the outer areas of the city were devastated. A quarter of a million Chinese died in the city in one month that year. With the founding of the People's Republic, in 1949, Mao Zedong settled on Beijing as his capital. Shanghai, which had been the most open, international and industrial of all China's cities, was kept under a tight rein. It served as the headquarters of the extreme left 'Gang of Four' in the 1960s and 1970s. But only when Shanghai was made a special economic zone in 1990 did the Bund start coming back to life – and regenerating and rebuilding some of its great waterfront buildings.

Liverpool and Shanghai both know one thing: they have some great and historic architecture – a crucial part of the fabric of modern cities – that is being adapted and redeveloped. That both cities appreciate the importance of this history is one of the strongest links between them.

The process of contemporary 'bonding' was confirmed a few years ago when Han Zheng, Mayor of Shanghai, wrote a foreword to the book *The Friendship Arch*, published to celebrate the twinning of the two cities; an event highlighted by the building – by highly skilled teams from Shanghai – of a magnificent Chinese arch in Liverpool's Chinatown, the oldest in Europe.

Mayor Han said: "We are gratified to see that Liverpool – a famous international maritime city – has made outstanding achievements in tourism, culture, education and sports. Shanghai is also committed to becoming a modern international metropolis and a global economic, financial, trade and shipping centre."

It is significant that Liverpool is showcasing its assets during the Shanghai Expo 2010, a programme shared by the Liverpool Shanghai Partnership, Liverpool Vision and other partners over a six–month–long event. In many ways it demonstrates the common ground between Liverpool and Shanghai; on the basis of two old friends who have much to talk about and a lot of ground to make up after a few years out of touch. They have a great future together.

*The stark outline of the Radio City tower in Liverpool city centre competes with the Liver Birds to stetch into the night sky.*

*A truly grand sight as the Royal Iris and Royal Daffodil cross mid–river, and in the background the Museum of Liverpool rises on the waterfront.*

# The Tale of Liverpool's Canal

**MARTIN CLARKE**
*Divisional Director, Jacobs*

IT is 1898 in a village in the jungle just inland from Georgetown, British Guyana in South America. The inhabitants are deeply superstitious, being descendants from West African slaves brought over as part of that great trade triangle that made many people wealthy, including, of course, the shipping merchants of Liverpool.

The witchdoctor in this particular village warns a young orphan he must leave the area because "he's different", and if he doesn't he'll be cursed. Terrified, the 14–year–old boy, called James Clarke, flees to the capital Georgetown, where he sneaks aboard a Russian timber ship. The ship sets sail for the other side of the world and first docks at Liverpool, where James gets off, starving and in rags. He spends a couple of days wandering the streets, suffering attacks from some of the bemused residents of late Victorian Liverpool, unused to seeing a black face amongst the teaming slums that stretched along and inland from the waterfront.

He is eventually taken in by Irish priests in north Liverpool and later adopted by a local family, the Crawfords. James grows up, works as a docker, gets married and has nine surviving children; others die as infants in the terrible poverty that people encountered in the infamous 'courts' – the slums in the north end of the city. He eventually becomes famous as a champion swimmer, who saved many lives in the docks where he worked and also near his home by the Leeds–Liverpool Canal, close to the Tate & Lyle sugar refinery. In those days children weren't taught to swim but, following James's efforts in hosting swimming lessons for local schools, swimming would eventually be taught to schoolchildren right across the city.

James died in 1946, but his memory lives on – he even had a street named after him in Vauxhall. There is also a plaque commemorating his life in the Eldonian community centre next to the canal, and there is a plaque in the entrance lobby of the Liverpool Aquatic Centre to celebrate his contribution to swimming in the city.

James Clarke was my granddad. So, apart from him, what's my link to the canal, the docks and the waterfront? Well, like his father before him, my dad, Mick Clarke, was a docker all his working life. However, as part of my own working life I would get the chance to be involved with a project that would transform the former workplace of my dad and granddad – the extension of the Leeds–Liverpool Canal along Liverpool's waterfront.

I first became involved in the canal extension project in 2003 when British Waterways appointed me as regeneration manager for the north: the canal link was my biggest project. The challenges I faced were huge. Amongst other problems, British Waterways had very little money to put towards the canal because their remit as a public corporation was to operate and maintain the existing network of canals and navigable rivers across the UK. And imagine the difficulties in getting planning consent to dig a new canal across the Pier Head on a World Heritage site.

Following a lot of sweat and tears we managed to persuade everyone that it was a project worth backing. Nearly £20 million of funding was secured from Government Office North West, the Northwest Regional Development Agency, English Partnerships and Peel Holdings. And we worked very hard with the city council's regeneration officers to come up with a design that would fit in with the city's most important piece of public realm at the Pier Head.

But why extend the canal? Well, it forms the focal point for the amazing transformation of the waterfront through Princes Dock, the Pier Head and at Mann Island. Also, by extending the canal network through the disused central docks to the north of the Pier Head and by bringing narrow boats and barges into the south docks, including the Albert Dock, the water space is brought back to life. And the impact that restored and rejuvenated canals can have on local communities and in regenerating the areas surrounding them can be seen in inner city areas right across Britain. Today, Liverpool is a 'destination' on the national canal network.

What would James Clarke have made of it all? It's hard for me to imagine how frightened he must have been as a starving and homeless stowaway aged 14 – the same age as my son James; and I worry if he gets the bus to town with his mates! I think my granddad would be amazed at the transformation of the waterfront.

He saved many lives directly and, by trailblazing swimming lessons in schools, he has saved many, many more indirectly. I can't match that, but I'd like to think that he'd be proud that the place where he landed, where he lived and where he worked all of his life, has been changed forever and that his grandson had a significant role in making it happen.

# Chapter 5

*Albert Dock*

*The light over Liverpool and the river Mersey is an ever–changing delight, transforming the mood almost minute by minute.*

*A photograph from 2004 looking across the Salthouse Dock, adjacent to the Albert Dock, takes in the imposing grandeur of the Port of Liverpool and Royal Liver buildings as the city begins to stir – a view no longer possible.*

# A Part of the Waterfront and City Fabric

Andrew Morris

*Director, Rathbones*

THERE is a certain piquancy attached to our firm having a base in the Port of Liverpool Building when looking at the history of the name Rathbone, which has a resonance in this city that echoes down through the ages from the early shipping trade and merchant activities of the 18th century to the present day, as one of the UK's leading provider of financial services.

Of course, apart from the great wealth created by astute commercial acumen, throughout its generations the family has demonstrated a philanthropic and campaigning character highlighted by William Rathbone IV's fierce opposition to Liverpool's involvement in the slave trade in the late 1700s. Then later that passion for social reform was epitomised by Eleanor Rathbone who after decade as the family traded in timber, salt, tobacco and a multitude of products including cotton. In fact, the records show that the firm imported the first cotton into Britain from the United States.

Then as expansion continued in the 1840s Samuel Greg Rathbone established two Chinese branch houses in Shanghai and Canton to purchase teas and silks in China and to export British goods to the Middle Kingdom. The branches were closed a decade or so later but the China trade continued very successfully with Rathbone Brothers becoming one of the largest tea importers to the UK.

Other trade links were forged with Egypt through the port of Alexandria and with South America where they dealt in coffee via Rio. In 1841 the firm became the Liverpool agents for the East India Company, dealing in textiles and cotton.

Towards the end of the 19th century Rathbones was faced with massive competition and found itself enmeshed in the difficulties traditional trading companies faced with the advance of steam power and telegraph communications. So critical was the situation that it was facing a profit loss for the first time in its history.

And so in what was then a seismic shift in both thinking and operations in 1912 the firm switched its emphasis from trading to the provision of financial services, which we have continued to this day.

In some ways it was inevitable. The family had generated considerable personal wealth through trading but had reached a stage where it was wondering which direction to take next. Managing money was the obvious route.

We like to believe that we are the oldest firm in Liverpool still operating in the same field – and obviously the same name running through 13 generations - and certainly there is a massive legacy that we carry with us.

The last William Rathbone – known affectionately as Bill – only retired from the main board of our plc company a few years ago and he was once a director of Ocean Transport and Trading that had its headquarters in Liverpool for many years. Those maritime associations to the original Rathbone line reminded us of how the company was founded – a quite unique history really.

Today we are maintaining the tradition of the old finance houses that existed in Liverpool during its maritime hey-day and our core base is still here. We now have over 800 people in UK locations that include Liverpool, London of course, Edinburgh and Winchester among others.

Here in Liverpool we actually have some 300 operational staff and manage over one and a half billions pounds of finance a year. We remain an independent house – there is no American or German bank behind the scenes or a South African parent company - and that helps us attract high quality individuals who want to exercise their investment flair and fund management skills. And we can actually find the high quality staff we need in this area, so it is perfect for us.

Liverpool is exceptionally strong in the business arena that we are in and there has been an influx of others 'players' to the city in recent years, which confirms our grasp of its relevance.

We also try to continue that Rathbone family caring ethos and Julian Rathbone is involved in the charity fund management side of our business.

Our location here on the waterfront is key to our image both in the UK and internationally. Its background in merchant trading and shipping imbues a sense of stability and we feel it gives the right message to our clients. In many ways we have come full circle: from a fundamental business trading model to private fund management services and still operating close to the river that was the source and inspiration for the original Rathbone entrepreneurs.

The company moved into the Port of Liverpool Building in 1984, as a planned expansion by Sebastian Rathbone who was a senior partner at the time. It was a significant move in many ways and when I joined in 1986 it was still a partnership. Since then we have expanded and transformed into a global player, we like to think of some distinction, with the overall group managing £11 billion of assets.

We now work on almost two floors of the building – all of the fourth and most of the third - and I am personally delighted as I have first hand views of the waterfront, which is almost embedded in my psyche. I was born in Liverpool and although I went away to university, I always felt the call to return home even when I was in London briefly, where everyone expects fund managers to be based.

But for me the capital wasn't the panacea and although Liverpool was enduring a tough patch in the 1980s it has been fantastic to see how the city has moved through a period of change, which has gained momentum in recent years.

My passion for the city and waterfront was influenced a lot by my father Roy who worked at Rathbones for fifty years, retiring as chief executive. But it was also his enthusiasm for the Mersey Partnership and promoting the city that equally fired me up. He was chairman of the Partnership for seven years and I have to confess his commitment did have an impact on how we all felt.

Liverpool is once again a vibrant place that can stand tall and proud. But of course, Rathbones has seen this city weather many political and economic storms and remained true. We never left and we are still here running a successful business.

In the 1990s the Canning Dock was a safe
haven for 'retired' tugs and 'lighters' in an
open air section of the Maritime Museum
– a view long since gone as development has
changed skylines and perspective.

# Spectacular Transition in Port's Fortunes

Frank Robotham

*Marketing Director, Peel Ports Group*

RENAISSANCE is one of those contemporary buzzwords that is so often misappropriated and over-worked. Frequently, the facts to which it is tagged just do not match the superlative. However, that cannot be said of its application to the city of Liverpool – and, more specifically, the port of Liverpool. Renaissance is the order of the day.

In the 1950s and 1960s the Liverpool waterfront mirrored the 'made in Britain' era and the UK's prominence as a leading exporter on the world trading scene. The port was a forest of ships' funnels and masts, protruding above dockside sheds accommodating an Aladdin's cave of cargoes. But global conditions changed, and so too the fortunes of the Mersey as a great maritime

I share the memories of those bygone days. I was a young lad, living less than half a mile from the docks in Bootle. I frequently played football on a green sward, which was to disappear some 30 years later to make way for Liverpool Freeport Park, one of the trail–blazing initiatives in the renaissance of the port of Liverpool.

Sunday afternoons were often spent with my parents riding the 'Dockers' Umbrella' overhead railway that ran the length of the north and south docks. The scenes were the truly magnificent stuff that memories are made of. They were gilded by the fact that there were few families in Liverpool who did not have members who worked on or sailed out of the docks. My own father – and grandfather before him – both sailed the north Atlantic as stewards on passenger ships with famous Cunard names such as the *Mauretania*.

At that time there were as many as 100 ships in the port of Liverpool on any given day. They would be there for as long as two or three weeks, discharging and loading a few thousand tonnes of the boxes, bags, barrels and bales that made up their general cargo. Today, the ships in port are far fewer. The people needed to discharge and load them have correspondingly diminished in number – all brought about by the advent of containerisation and mechanised bulk handling. The modern container ship will discharge and load as much cargo as four or five of the old general cargo ships in 10 hours – not days. The grain that was once delivered in manhandled bags is now offloaded mechanically at a rate of 1,800 tonnes an hour. Today, fewer ships are in and out in a fraction of the time, but carrying many times the volume of cargo.

Who would have predicted that, less than half a century on, the Port of Liverpool, against all odds and forecasts, would have bucked predictions to handle not just as much cargo as in those memorable days, but more than at any time in its history – nearly 34 million tonnes of the most diverse range of freight to be found in any UK port... containers, forest products, grain, steel, scrap metal for recycling, oils, cocoa, coal, chemicals, roll–on roll–off freight and, of course, people – crossing the Irish Sea or as passengers sailing away on the increasing number of cruise ships calling into the Mersey.

Those luxury floating palaces calling at the Pier Head's landing stage or docking at West Langton cruise terminal give the mighty Mersey a splash of the glamour so glowingly recalled from the days when the way to travel the world was not by jumbo jet, but by sea, aboard elegant ocean liners. But the majestic passenger ships of today are just the sparkling surface of a spectacular transition in the fortunes of the port and, consequently, the city. It was a change achieved by the work of many over nearly 30 years, from the beginning of the 1980s, and one which rescued the relationship between river and city.

There was a time when the love affair between Liverpool and its waterfront began to cool, when the city turned its back on the river and the decline and strife with which it had become associated. It was not rejection by the city council, but by the community at large, who seemed to share the conviction that the port no longer offered a future... no longer had a role in the regeneration of their city.

I am pleased to say we have put the romance back into that relationship – as spectacularly illustrated by the Tall Ships event in 2008 – a combined operation of city and port that provided the people of Liverpool and beyond a sight that was the stuff of new memories.

When the Tall Ships first visited Liverpool in 1984, the transition of the port from decline to success was in its early stages. It was handling a meagre nine million tonnes of cargo after going through a tectonic shift in fortune. When I worked for Blue Funnel and Elder Dempster Lines after leaving school their operations and influence were global, encompassing the Far East, Australasia, South Africa and more. But, at about the same time, Liverpool was in the midst of industrial unrest, which hung huge question marks over the port's prospects. Combined with the advent of containerisation, it heralded the need for radical change in the industry.

Just as I was beginning to conclude that there were better career prospects outside the shipping industry, the Mersey Docks & Harbour Company advertised for "an economist, with a marketing role". The economist's job lasted about half a day because I didn't know why they needed an economist and I wasn't an economist. But the marketing role continued for three years until I was appointed personal assistant to the managing director, Jim Fitzpatrick. I was in the job for four years, the latter part of which was spent preparing the case for the Port of Liverpool to be one of Britain's first pioneer free zones. We came up on the outside to secure one of the six licences issued by Margaret Thatcher, thanks to the support of people like Malcolm Thornton, the then MP for Crosby, whose backing was pivotal to our success. Given the job of putting theory into practice as the Freeport manager, I had the pleasure of totally trashing the case put by doubters such as journalist Roger Eglin in his letter to Mrs Thatcher, published in the *Sunday Times* the weekend after the Freeport winners were announced. More than 20 years after their predictions that Liverpool Freeport was doomed to fail, it is still the UK's most successful free zone.

The Freeport opened in November 1984 and the first 20–ft container of free zone goods – tyre tubes bound for Kirkby Tyres – arrived from Korea one dark afternoon just before Christmas. We put in a request for three dockers and a forklift truck to unload the box. The dockers refused to do the work but intervention by Jimmy Symes, the full–time official of the Transport & General Workers' Union, saw them back on the job; the box was unloaded and the Freeport was in business.

Jimmy was a real character among characters on the docks. In his later years, he was also a key figure in the stabilisation of industrial relations in the port, which was the foundation for Liverpool's future success.

In 1989 Mrs Thatcher opened Liverpool Freeport Park, a development that buried my childhood football pitch forever, but marked a major milestone in the progress of what is, today, Britain's largest and most successful free zone. Six hundred thousand square feet of established quayside sheds were converted into warehousing for the Freeport within the first four years. But we needed yet more space. The 40,000 sq ft of Freeport Park warehousing was the first speculative development of business units by Mersey Docks. Today, there is more than four million sq ft of warehousing within the boundary of the port and Freeport, which was extended at Liverpool and Birkenhead under the Wirral and Sefton City Challenge schemes. Companies who left the docks to avoid the strictures of the old Dock Labour Scheme have now returned, to join others who recognise the merits of being within one of Britain's busiest and most dynamic ports.

But the success of Liverpool Freeport could not have been achieved without the backing of other key people such as senior customs officers Jack Mulcahy and David Jones. If you didn't have 'Customs' at your side, you were lost; just as you were lost if you didn't have Jimmy Symes recognising what you were trying to achieve.

There have been other key factors which have contributed to and are still building on the success of the Port of Liverpool – the Twelve Quays terminal for Irish Sea ferries at Birkenhead, right opposite Pier Head; the resurgence of Cammell Laird; the development of the cruise trade; the first privately owned Channel Tunnel rail terminal in the UK; the return of most of the UK's cocoa trade after an absence of 30 years; and the push for the return of what was another major trade years back, with the construction of a new terminal for fresh produce. All this, underpinned throughout by the largest maritime community outside London.

As marketing director of the Peel Ports Group, which acquired the Port of Liverpool along with the rest of Mersey Docks, I can look back at a phenomenal period of change and achievement – and look forward to the implementation of yet more plans for success.

None carries the significance of our plans to develop a second container terminal, on the river rather than in the docks, and capable of accommodating the new post–Panamax generation of larger container ships. This £100–million–plus investment is the key to the next quantum leap in the development not just of the Port of Liverpool, but further up–river, the expansion of the Manchester Ship Canal. With these two historic rivals merged under the Peel Ports banner, the exciting opportunity has been created for a continuous water highway for international trade. Stretching from Royal Seaforth Dock at the mouth of the Mersey to the heart of the largest industrial region outside London, this 'green' route culminates in Peel's planned multi–million–pound Port Salford intermodal terminal at the eastern end of the Ship Canal, adding yet more momentum to the evident renaissance of the Port of Liverpool and its river.

'There was a time when the love affair between Liverpool and its waterfront began to cool, when the city turned its back on the river and the decline and strife with which it had become associated'

*The corner of the Maritime Museum in Jesse Hartley's gloriously restored Albert Dock, which was originally opened in 1846 and now incorporates the largest group of Grade 1 listed buildings in the UK.*

# Living at the Edge of Everyday Life

CATHY ROBERTS
*Founder 'Bespoke' Storytelling Company*

THE river ran away with me when I was four years old. As I sat on Crosby beach at the Mersey's mouth, watching for ships, the rushing tide raced past and carried me out to the sea of dreams. Nobody noticed, primarily because in the shortened sight of adults I was still sitting in Castle Cockle, my private fortress.

But I knew I'd sailed away, further than the faintest foghorns, where tide takes over from time.

Forty years later, and the tides still guide my life. The childhood dream of steering past the Pier Head at the wheel of my own ship came true when I brought my 70–year–old Yarwood's tug *France–Hayhurst* around the northern British coast from Yorkshire's river Aire to Liverpool's Albert Dock.

I spent two years of my life, and all associated savings, restoring this much neglected and wrecked riverboat to sea–going splendour. Far too big for the straightforward canal, sea–going was what she had to be, wryly defined by one cynical sea dog as: "Seagoing? You just fix her up and see how she goes."

If the restoration – which sounds unsuitably grand for what is still very much a tough old tug – was a challenge, the process of conveying this rejuvenated old lady around the coast proved to be as heart–stopping as any adventure I had conjured as a child. The North Sea threw us about – me and a crew of ancient mariners – for three disconcerting days and nights, while the Irish Sea paid us even less respect.

Whirlpools are no longer only experienced in my imagination. The terrifying turmoil of 10 days of high winds and waves, and shredded nerves, were suddenly calmed, as Liverpool Bay's Bar Light appeared through the murky autumnal first light. All the sailors' stories I had ever heard suddenly made sense – I'd seen the light many times in other people's boats, but it's different from your own vessel. Once you see the coast, and enter the channel, the excitement threatens to throw you off–course, as you see the familiar landmarks as though for the first time. The 'Dome of Home' – SS Peter and Paul's Church in New Brighton, Perch Rock and finally, momentarily obscured by the recent intrusive skyscraper skyline, the Liver Birds, hailing us home.

Finally feeling for the first time that I am where I should be, in a vintage tug boat moored at what is I believe the most atmospheric area of the city, I am living at the edge of everyday life, watching with interest the tidal streams of visitors, workers and residents who parade around the dock – some oblivious to the river and its business. Property developers with a visible self–importance patrol alongside parents and children in search of pirates; tourists stroll under the arched former warehouses, sometimes stopping to stare at the boats. A lot of people stare without seeing anything. I look up from the wheelhouse to see somebody looking straight through me. An apparent apparition, I don't seem to materialise until I step out on deck. And then my most mundane of movements provides instant fascination. Quite often whole conversations, running commentaries, are conducted about my ship and me. I used to chip in, usually to settle the countless debates about the origin of the boat, until I realised that to a great many people I am still invisible. So many people these days look without seeing.

First and last light at the Albert Dock is what I love best. When the sun first breaks in through the buildings and cloaks the walls with a warm shell pink glow, and the silence sings. On summer mornings there's usually a good two to three hours before the rest of the world butts in. And in the evening, it's that early indigo that seeps from the sky into the water washed in from the river. It's then that the real ghosts go about their business. For a short while you can see the bustling warehouses, and hear the great warps straining, and hear the same unfamiliar accents that echo around the dock in the daytime, but which now in the darkness sound softer and more intriguing.

And when I climb below decks, into my bed built in the bow of the boat, I lie listening to the gently splashing waves around the hull, and the rush of the tide beyond the dock. And I know that I am home.

When I sailed past Crosby beach, into the wide–open mouth of the river, I glanced over at the vast yawning sands. Iron Men now stand where I sat as a child, staring just as defiantly out at a promising sea, waiting for the racing tide to carry them away. And I know where they're going.

*The Albert Dock – which was still partially operational until the early 1960s – is today one of the top tourist attractions in the UK.*

# Thresholds to the Ends of the Earth

**STEPHEN BROADBENT**
*Sculptor and Artist*

MY own journey as a sculptor owes a great deal to my mentor Arthur Dooley, who in the early 60s, rather than getting the bus to start the early shift at the Dunlop factory, instead crossed the road and caught the bus to the Pier Head, where he stood looking out to the Mersey to declare: "Today I am a sculptor." Then he went home, told his dad, bought a weld set and began his astonishing career.

The Mersey waterfront is a place for such declarations: it's the trumpet mouthpiece of the city, a place to announce to the world who and what we are, and what we hold dear.

My remembrance as a child is not of a seaport crammed with ships and ocean liners, bustling with dockers, but instead a wonderful, derelict Albert Dock structure, a playground with a jaded beauty that has not been surpassed by its restoration.

Liverpool's particular genetic code has been transmuted somehow into its materiality; its colour, scale and the forms that have been built. The built environment tells the Liverpool story and even today, after eight centuries of economic ups and downs, people continue to leave their mark on the waterfront.

It is hard to conceive the mindset behind a transport plan to raze the Albert Dock structure to the ground to serve as a car park for a motorway that would have decisively split the city from the waterfront. So I am thankful that there were those who had the imagination to see that the waterfront held the key to the city's future, as it had been the reason for its birth.

As a young aspiring artist I continued to be fascinated by the waterfront, particularly the remnants of the Princes Dock structure; with its decayed timbers opening up to the scary tidal water it was an eerie place and so evocative of Liverpool's past. The stories of travellers to and from the New World inspired me, years later, to design the *Face of Liverpool* gardens on Old Hall Street, with the slogan cut into the weathering steel wall 'Liverpool – Threshold to the Ends of the Earth'.

The waterfront is a threshold place, the front room of the city, spruced up to meet and greet the world, and where once Arthur Dooley's red 'Tatlinesque' tower celebrated the working people of this city and trades unionism, a unique artwork now sadly demolished.

One of my favourite sculptures on the waterfront is the granite *Memorial to the Engine Room Heroes* inspired by the 32 engineers of the *Titanic* who stayed at their posts to keep the ship afloat long enough to man the lifeboats. The sculptor was Goscombe John and it was unveiled in 1916. I love the composition of the obelisk, with the heroic figures carved in high–relief, holding shovels and spanners, and four Rodinesque crouching figures at each corner symbolising the four elements, and the gilded torch, commemorative of those that kept the lights burning.

Time inevitably flies, and lives change with it. Now the waterfront becomes a place to take the kids, often via a wonderful bicycling adventure from Otterspool promenade to the Pier Head.

We always took visitors to the waterfront, and had to make a pilgrimage to the decorative architecture of the Mersey Tunnel ventilation towers, which the zealous modernists accused of being a deplorable architectural sham, but to our post–modern sensibilities are seen as great fun; a pick and mix of exotic influences and styles from all over the world. What a wonderful indulgence, emerging as a result of the austerity of the Great War and such an optimistic celebration of the machine age. The sculptor was the Liverpool–based Edmund Thompson.

One of my own public artworks celebrates the connections between the melody and the lyrics to the hymn *Amazing Grace* written in 1772 by the one–time slaveship captain, John Newton. He later became a tide surveyor for the Customs & Excise office in Liverpool and then a Church of England minister.

The hymn is said to be the most recorded song in the world and sung publicly at least 10 million times a year. It was written with no tune in mind, and it was only in 1835 that the lyrics connected to the now familiar melody. This union of lyrics and melody – merged through the Afro–American gospel culture of the southern US states, ironically by descendants of slaves that Newton had probably transported in his early life – popularised the hymn throughout the world.

My work is located appropriately enough at the ferry terminal building on the Pier Head, embracing the travellers and waterfront promenaders and within reach of the river, and thus the wider continents linked by the seas.

*The summer of 2008 and the Salthouse Dock is a big draw for tall ships' fans. In the background the construction work at the Pier Head continues.*

The changing face of King's Dock – the £64 million convention centre and 10,000 seat arena at Monarch Quay epitomises Liverpool's rapid development into a 21st century city.

# Last Night I Dreamed I Went to 'Sailortown'

## Susan Hanley–Place MBE

*Honorary Chief Executive, The Mersey Heritage Trust*

AS old Victoria retired to her bed at Windsor, the tides of the world were flooding into Liverpool, second city of her Empire. The Mersey, sliding in like pewter, disgorged sailing ships into the dock–mouths. Towed between the granite quays, jib–booms vaulting from carved clipper bows, 'high canvas' rig towering above salt–washed decks, they crowded, clanged and negotiated unloading positions, a forest of masts against the Mersey sunset smudged by the smoke of puffer tugs and dock engines, flaring in the deep windows of sail–lofts capturing the last light.

Long, massive carts swarmed to the quays, iron rims on stone booming like artillery through the warehouse alleys. Hundreds of huge, heavy horses, hooves the size of dinner plates, standing ready, snuffling 'chop' from nosebags, waiting the inexorable sway and thump of cargo nets coming ashore begins. The gathering night crowd not spectators but shipping agents, clerks, wharfingers and labourers, intent on documenting, counting, loading and distributing cargo into warehouses. Liverpool works the night under the command of the rolling heartbeat of the tides.

The ships have made their formidable sea passages for one reason only. Cargo, trade, and commerce: the lifeblood of Liverpool, the cement between the stones of St George's Hall, the foundations of merchant mansions in her gracious parks, the source of her lavish flowering of fine architecture.

Last of all, when their ship's hold is an echoing emptiness, her yards squared away, her sails in harbour–stow and she warped away to allow another vessel to the quay, a reeking, raggedy group of men staggers down a plank to set their shaky feet on shore. They are stone cold sober but some of them fall on the cobbles, others pick them up and they weave their way like a many–legged creature, signed off and heading for the Red Lion, the Trawler, the Baltic Fleet and oblivion from heaving decks. People step from the shadows to meet them. Sometimes family have come to take them home. Often, a ship is their only home and a soft strange womanly arm slipped into theirs speaks of safe haven for a while.

These are the men who made Liverpool. They are your great–grandfathers. Raw courage is the sweat of men pushed to their extremes. If you met them swaying along the Strand

at 03.00 hours on that chilly 1890 morning, reeking of Stockholm Tar and bilges, you would pass on the other side of the road. I would, too, though I am one of a few dozen people in Liverpool who has shared any of their experience. I have always stood with the 'Sons of Martha', but would not presume to walk alongside those heroes.

When I came to live in Liverpool, in 1968, echoes of 'high canvas' still hung around the waterfront. I drank beer and sang shanties in old 'Sailortown' pubs; traditional music led me into the muscular heartlands of the north docks: to Oily Joes, the Long Bar, and the A1 at Lloyds.

Mingling with waterfront men, I met an identity independent of the modern mantras of money and status. They called themselves 'Scousers' after a rough sailors' stew. Their heroes were grandfathers who went to sea on sailing ships, self–reliant survivors who had ridden the dangerous winds of the world and shrugged at the lesser hardships of the land. In the brotherhood of the fo'c'sle the currency of respect was capability, life–threatening challenges were tackled with ironic humour, and a shipmate was someone you never let down. In neighbourhoods where every household had men away at sea, capable pragmatic women held home and community together. The formidable personality of a seafaring community was the bedrock of the Scouse identity.

In my first fortnight in Liverpool I wore out a new pair of shoes walking around, just looking. The mud–filled magnificence of Albert, Wapping,

Herculaneum; hundreds of original Armstrong hydraulic machines, iron beasts asleep in the weeds. A Gothic fantasia of pumping stations, gatehouses, ashlar–faced quays stretching along miles of waterfront. The daughter of an engineer and an artist, I recognised the legacy of men who knew the beauty of a marriage between function and form.

But I had arrived as a fierce destructive squall swept in. Visigoth horsemen galloping through throwing torches into roofs could have wreaked no more ignorant destruction than the carelessness with which the last inheritance of Liverpool 'Sailortown' was wasted in the 1970s. The stumps of the Overhead Railway already stood like rotted teeth along the Dock Road. With an astonishing lack of foresight, waterfront weints and alleys of Georgian sail–lofts were cleared away. But a mark in the sand was stepped over when the awesome Sailors' Home was demolished.

When I first encountered Liverpool's dockland community there was already a growing sense of loss. Neighbourhoods dismantled, landmarks derelict; planning decisions many people disagreed with. These things happen – social and economic priorities shift, familiar backgrounds are replaced; the process of redevelopment is seldom popular. Redevelopment with a firm sense of vision and sure hands on the helm is a revitalising force, but as the decade drew on, Liverpool increasingly resembled a ship with her wheel lashed at the helm whilst arguments over captaincy raged below–decks.

The ripple of anger around the empty socket of the Sailors' Home was the first twitch in the hide of an awakening giant; recognition that mediocre minds must be opposed. Failure to perceive widening chasms between planning and people is an endemic failing of government. When the massive, spectacular landmark of Albert Dock was earmarked to make way for a car park, a bellow of: "Not on your bloody life" went up. We felt like terriers snapping at heels, but the communal chorus voiced an alarm call which caught the attention of the new Minister for Merseyside.

Michael Heseltine was good for Liverpool. The 'privateer' panache that hung about 'Hezza' appealed to Scousers. He sailed on gut instincts, assessing chances, finding the weather–gauge. People were persuaded to re–voice ideas which had been dismissed as dreams. His new vessel, the Merseyside Development Corporation, had a government 'Letter of Marque' to bring in a 'prize' for Liverpool – tourism.

Liverpool's potential to attract international visitors had been so patently obvious to anyone who took the time to research historic seaport regeneration that the Development Corporation's tourism agenda caused a sigh of relief rather than surprise. If a muddy creek in New England could be reborn as 'Mystic Seaport', Liverpool had a winning hand to play.

I had time in the early 1980s to reflect on waterfront regeneration. Working on the Docklands History project, I walked miles each day through the south docks photographing buildings and architectural details before demolition. The physical structure of the waterfront was now in hands with serious money; my thoughts turned to how to revitalise its courageous, resilient identity.

Mersey Heritage Trust began with a white cat sitting in the lap of a veteran judge. In the bare–knuckle ring of Liverpool politics, *The Joker* and *The Riddler* were in temporary charge. On BBC Radio Merseyside I said we needed to regain Liverpool's true identity, and spoke of reviving the May Horse Parade. Next day, the Lord Mayor's coachman hitched a coach and pair to a lamppost in the street outside and came looking for me. Now I sat in his harness room with Sir Sanderson Temple, the Recorder of Liverpool, and a cluster of old carters, Victorian leather and Liver Bird buckles gleaming in the shadows. Militants had locked away Liverpool's 'state coach' as a symbol of privilege. "The coach is actually the symbol that every docker's son or daughter can become the 'First Citizen' of Liverpool," mused Sir Sanderson. "If you want to do this parade, m'dear, there are many with you." The following May, we processed a mile of gorgeously decorated horses led by the 'state coach' from Sefton Park to St George's Hall; tens of thousands stood as if witnessing a vision and told their grandchildren: "This is the real Liverpool."

The Dock Company's chairman, Jim Fitzpatrick, was in the crowd. "What can you do with a dock?" he wondered. At Stanley Dock our new charity conducted a heritage experiment.

Heritage is not about nostalgia but investment in the future. It maintains the depth and richness of community identity. Revitalising cherished aspects of community life sends ripples into the future, sowing seeds, shifting thinking. Dockland festivals bringing fleets of canal boats down a disused waterway gave British Waterways new food for thought. Our Heritage Market shifted the Stanley Dock from derelict demolition candidate to listed building waiting for new purpose.

The tide was sliding in again. As we experimented with community education, worked with volunteer teams and learned how to tackle formidable problems, a brigantine – the *Zebu* – was then circumnavigating the world, and she would put our practice to the test. When *Zebu* returned to retire from the towering cloud–mountains of the 'Trades', it was to Liverpool, into the care of Mersey Heritage and a home berth at Albert Dock. Hundreds of people from teens to 80–year–olds helped rebuild her, learning sailormen's skills, passing the legacy of 'high canvas' into the future.

History never stands still. It is the sound of the night wind on the sea, not a monument planted on the land. We should not haunt the ruins of the past. But sometimes ordinary people need to gather up what matters, shoulder the burden between them, and make sure that their grandchildren will see a May Horse garlanded with flowers, a tower of 'high canvas' in the dawn, an awesome building put to new use. These are the legacies of the Liverpool waterfront.

'In neighbourhoods where every household had men away at sea, capable pragmatic women held home and community together. The formidable personality of a seafaring community was the bedrock of the Scouse identity'

Nothing dwarfs the Cathedral Church of Christ, designed by Sir Giles Gilbert Scott and which is the largest cathedral in Britain. King Edward VII laid the foundation stone on 19 July 1904 and building was finally completed on 25 October 1978. It was marked by a service attended by Queen Elizabeth II. In the foreground a 'temple' to the modern gods of music and commerce now completes a visually stunning waterfront.

# Chapter 6

## Urban Reflections

*A view of Liverpool from Bidston Hill, which rises some 125 metres above Wirral and looks down on the Radio City tower, a mere 77 metres high, and the Metropolitan Cathedral of Christ the King, designed by Sir Frederick Gibberd and consecrated in 1967.*

*The 'shell' of the Museum of Liverpool rises at the Pier Head, a building that dramatically changes the traditional image of the waterfront forever.*

# The Reassuring Ebb and Flow of the River

**Christoph Grunenberg**
*Director, Tate Liverpool*

WHEN I moved to Liverpool to take up the position of director at Tate Liverpool, in the spring of 2001, it was a radically different city to the one it is now – not just in its physical appearance but also in the mood that was prevailing in Liverpool. Travelling from London on an old train on a dark and wet November day, I was at times apprehensive and wondered if this was indeed the right move. These were the days before the award of the European Capital of Culture and massive investment into the city. However, once I settled in Liverpool, the city cast the familiar spell that keeps natives as well as outsiders in its thrall.

It often feels that Tate Liverpool has grown up with Liverpool, its development reflecting the changing fortunes of the city, from the darkest days of industrial decline and the political turmoil of the 1980s to the triumphant celebration of the Capital of Culture in 2008. An important milestone was the major expansion of the building in 1998, providing much needed additional exhibition space. Today, I believe that the gallery is a cultural beacon for Liverpool and the Albert Dock, many visitors making the trip to the city especially to visit Tate Liverpool. In a city like Liverpool it is possible to effect change to a much greater degree than it might be in a metropolitan centre. It is particularly in places that for decades have been marginalised that arts organisations can realise their full potential: they can be engines of regeneration and renewal; they provide a sense of place and identity; and they foster creativity and expression.

When the Tate Trustees first thought about a Tate in the north, they talked of an 'outstation' and 'branch', terms no longer applied to Tate Liverpool today. The Tate's first site outside London has become an independent and internationally respected institution with its own distinct profile, much envied by many other cities. Tate was not only pioneering in its commitment to establish a site outside the capital, but also in using a former industrial space, one of the first of many art galleries and museums around the world to do so. Tate Gallery Liverpool – as it was then called – opened in May 1988 in an historic 1840s Albert Dock warehouse converted by James Stirling. Its first exhibition was the inspirational *Starlit Waters*, featuring the works of some of Britain's finest sculptors such as Richard Long, Michael Craig–Martin, Richard Deacon and Antony Gormley, as well as the memorable display of Mark Rothko's *Seagram* murals. I attended the opening of Tate Liverpool in 1988 as a student, never imagining that one day I would be the gallery's director.

It is significant that Tate Liverpool is so connected with the sea – our nearest neighbour – so important in the city's history and continuing to shape its image and outlook. One of the reasons for establishing a Tate gallery in Liverpool was, of course, the fortuitous lineage that could be drawn to Henry Tate's original sugar company, founded here in the 19th century. The Albert Dock is part of the UNESCO World Heritage site celebrating Liverpool's maritime and trading heritage. This has been formative in defining the city's international perspective and openness to outside influences – qualities and principles we feel we can relate to and which have guided the gallery's work over the past two decades.

The twin pillars of Tate's programme have always been the presentation of the national collection of modern and contemporary art and its special exhibitions. Thousands of visitors come every week to see extraordinary works by artists ranging from Rodin to Warhol, Picasso to Hirst, in extensive and ever–changing displays from the Tate's rich holdings. Exhibitions have brought the best of British and international art from all over the globe to Liverpool.

The gallery has demonstrated a flair for risk and experimentation, staging many pioneering exhibitions that introduced artists for the first time to a wider audience or traced particular themes in 20th–century art. Highlights have included Salvador Dalí, *Shopping: A Century of Art and Consumer Culture*, *Summer of Love* and the presentation of the Turner Prize 2007, the first time in its history that the award has been staged outside London.

We welcome an average of 600,000 visitors annually, though in the Capital of Culture year it was closer to a million. The exhibition *Gustav Klimt: Painting, Design and Modern Life in Vienna 1900* has broken all our previous visitor records, firmly placing Liverpool on the international map as a destination. We remain a gallery shaped by its local environment and deeply appreciated by the local population. I feel proud that I have been part of the remarkable transformation that Liverpool has undergone over the past decade and that I have been able personally to make a contribution.

A gaggle of the much-loved offspring of Superlambanana, the iconic statue by Japanese sculptor Taro Chiezi, that seemed to take over the whole of Liverpool in the summer of 2008, and became a cult into the bargain. These cute little 'beasties' were located close to the waterfront and gaze out towards the river as though seeking sight of the old Fyffes banana boats that would dock opposite.

*The Liverpool One site takes shape with the outline of the Cammell Laird shipyard sheds in the background and then further views across Wirral take in the rolling Welsh hills.*

# Changing Faces
## Then and Now on the Liverpool Waterfront

Peter Morton

*Director, Mersey Waterfront*

LIVERPOOL'S waterfront is without doubt one of the most varied and dramatic landscapes in the North West of England. Over the years, of course, it has changed along with the economic and social development of the city.

My own first recollections of the waterfront go back to the mid 1950s – rides on the Overhead Railway and family days out on the ferry to New Brighton. I even have a print on the wall at home of Wirral 'slate' artist Brian Gordon's well–loved work *The Day Out* showing those wonderful trips up the river on the old ferry boats.

On a professional basis I have worked in economic business development and investment for most of my career. I can still remember the heartbreaking trek along the south docks in the late 1970s, looking to find businesses that we could help to develop to try to redress the catastrophic decline in the local economy. It is easy to forget how desolate the landscape was – unless of course you are lucky enough to own

That television series was highly acclaimed for its powerful and emotional depiction of the desperation inflicted by high unemployment, and recorded the human impact of the physical decline that resulted from the disappearance of Liverpool's traditional employers.

The challenges facing Liverpool 30 years ago were immense. We endured some rather difficult times in the 1970s, 1980s and 1990s but – through hard work and colossal investment – the picture has changed quite dramatically. Along the way we have had to change perceptions and raise our ambitions. But it hasn't all been straightforward.

In the early 1980s I was working for the then Merseyside County Council in its economic development arm, MERCEDO. We dreaded Fridays because it seemed that, come the end of the week, another major factory closure would be announced. The city and its business base were almost entirely dependent on waterfront – or should I say port–related – business. The docks and the industries that processed the raw materials imported into the country had been the major employers for decades.

At school in the late 1960s our careers advice was based on the city's history rather than its future prospects. So I was told to go into insurance, because that was a safe and secure job with one of the city's major employers. Insurance and many other traditional employment sectors and businesses have long since departed, largely because Liverpool's economy was based on a branch office structure, with few Liverpool–owned businesses.

After gaining an economics and geography degree I worked in advertising and consumer protection, before joining MERCEDO. We had two key strategies: try to get new businesses started – largely by offering financial incentives – and try to encourage overseas companies to relocate to Merseyside. One of our key events was an annual trip to the Hanover Messe, one of Europe's largest trade fairs, with over 200,000 visitors. In those days, the Government had created the Merseyside Development Corporation (MDC) to lead the regeneration of the waterfront, initially the south docks and the Liverpool waterfront.

As part of our trip to Hanover in 1982 we took a four–metre by two–metre model of the planned developments and paid for a Merseyside supplement in the German edition of the *Financial Times*. As the supplement was written in German we paid little attention to it until, on about the fifth day of the exhibition, it was pointed out that MDC had unfortunately used rather ill–considered wording in their quarter–page advert. It read: "The last major change to the south docks in Liverpool was planned by Adolf Hitler." Not necessarily the best advert to use in Germany!

The historic identity gives character to our waterfront, from the World Heritage site at Liverpool's Pier Head to the wide–ranging nature reserves and Sites of Special Scientific Interest.

I can remember going to see the last tram depart from the Pier Head in 1957, on its last journey to the Edge Lane sheds. After that, the area in front of the Liver Buildings became a bus station. And I still remember the terrible old joke – Question: "Does this bus stop at the Pier 'ed?" Answer: "I 'ope so mate, or there'll be a big splash!"

Like many of the developments in the 1960s that bus station became the epitome of the worst developments in the world: grey concrete, horrible off–white tile mosaic cladding, desolate kiosks, a café that was the 'greasiest spoon' in the world and a sub–culture of homeless itinerants, who chose to use the public areas as toilets. This was Liverpool at its worst – not so much unsafe as unpleasant – and not what we would hold out as a jewel in any crown!

Seeing the Pier Head become a wonderful piazza – with that desolate bus station confined to memory – was the first step into making what is now the world–famous World Heritage site, and was one of the first signs of Liverpool's commitment to a bright future.

If you type the year 1984 into a search engine it tells you about the George Orwell book that relates the harrowing tale of an all–knowing government using pervasive and constant surveillance of the populace, insidious and blatant propaganda and brutal control over its citizens. It was a work of fiction – and yet some would say that the government of the day in the UK tried to exert its influence through insidious and blatant propaganda and strict, if not brutal, control over its citizens.

But in 1984 Liverpool also saw the first visit of the Tall Ships and, of course, the International Garden Festival. It was a fabulous summer and one which showed what can be done to inspire confidence. Unfortunately, we didn't have the gumption to build on that confidence and preserve the fabulous gardens on the Garden Festival site. So now we have to spend more money restoring them to their former glory.

Now, again, the area surrounding the Pier Head has undergone major development. A new canal link, a new ferry terminal, a new museum, substantial commercial and residential development and a new piazza along and above the canal are all part of the visionary approach, which includes features such as Canadian Maple trees and a smaller but much valued green space surrounding the cleaned up statue of Edward VII on his horse.

Many people criticised the development undertaken in 2008, the city's year as European Capital of Culture. But the overall plan involved substantially more than the £100 million investment into the development and redevelopment of new and existing buildings. And everyone has to agree that it is a major – and magnificent – change from the days when we had the world's worst bus station!

Naturally, developing the Liverpool and Mersey waterfront is a long–term project. The revitalisation is an ongoing process that started with public funding but is also a partnership with private sector capital.

Inevitably, some of that work has involved revitalising areas that were neglected, given that we see public access as a prerequisite of our work. And, over the long term, developing a sustainable coast – both in economic and environmental terms – will be achieved by planning in public and private partnerships and engaging the public through participation in the planning and designs.

For me, personally, the chance of leading the development of the Mersey Waterfront Regional Park – to give it its full title – is a hugely exciting challenge. Much work has been undertaken to improve and secure the quality of water and the environment along the coastline of the river Mersey. This was, in many respects, the first stage of the regeneration process; to make sure that our communities can enjoy the waterfront as part of the existing urban fabric.

The most famous location on the Mersey is, perhaps, the Liverpool waterfront area that takes in the Pier Head – it is a global brand in its own right and is recognised internationally. There has been a dramatic change in the way it looks, even from just a decade ago, and I believe we are witnessing the creation of an enhanced waterfront experience of international repute.

Our job was – and is – to promote and animate the waterfront with events and we are keen to install public art alongside the river to enhance the visitor experience. We also work with

Mersey Ferries to, hopefully, extend the scope of the cruises to take in other locations – such as New Brighton, once a great seaside attraction by ferry from Liverpool – journeys I recall with such fondness from my own youth.

We have also worked closely with a range of partners to develop a long–term River of Light to illuminate key buildings and allow for night–time animation, spectacular lighting sculptures and other fascinating features – maybe even a 'bridge of light' linking Liverpool to the Wirral.

All in all, it's just another brick in the wall!

'The city and its business base were almost entirely dependent on waterfront – or should I say port-related – business. The docks and the industries that processed the raw materials imported into the country had been the major employers for decades'

The original Superlambanana, *here located outside this demolished ships' chandlers, which was at one point owned by former Liverpool Lord Mayor Trevor Jones.*

*Dusk falls over the Liverpool One construction
site in February 2008.*

# Regarding King John and Other Matters

**VICTOR ASHLEY**
*Entrepreneur and owner of Park Lodge*

AS a boy I would scramble around the quaysides and warehouses of the south docks with my mates, scouring the ground for the loose peanuts spilled from the canvas–bagged cargoes of ships from faraway places that I knew little about. I am, after all, Liverpool born and bred. But, in fact, some distant lands are an essential part of my own past. My father was a merchant seaman, a stoker, from Freetown in Sierra Leone – and his father the descendant of freed slaves who had fought for the British in the American War of Independence.

On a journey to Liverpool in World War II a German submarine attacked his ship and he fell down a steel ladder and snapped his leg. It meant he had to recuperate for a longer time than usual and find semi–permanent accommodation in the city. That was difficult then as there was a mindset abroad that outrageously declared: "No Irish, no 'Blacks' and no dogs". He found lodgings with my mother, Mary Ashley, and they became, as the expression goes, friendly, and soon had set up home together.

But, as a long time mariner he was a bit restless and fond of wandering; I think that is the euphemism. As a result he and my mother eventually parted and I would only see him when he returned to Liverpool after another seagoing trip. I recall he was a snappy dresser and a very handsome man, with a memorable name: Victor Melvyn Hedd. It sounds kind of Norwegian but clearly isn't considering his origins in west Africa – or maybe it is; all sailors get about a bit. He settled in Liverpool when he retired and asked me to change my family name to his, but I'd been brought up by my mother and wanted to stay loyal to her.

When I was 16 I did have a notion to 'go to sea' myself – I think every lad in Liverpool had this idea at one point in those days – and tried to sign up as a cabin boy or deckhand on the big liners. One day I went with a friend to Mann Island to pursue this dream. I was upset at the time when my friend got a job and I didn't.

But then, if I'd sailed away I probably wouldn't have met my wife Paula – whose family, Lynch, actually hails from another dispossessed Diaspora, those forced to flee the Great Famine of Ireland in the 18th century. We got married – in the face of some opposition, I must admit – and a few years later we started buying property, to rent or sell. If we hadn't been entrepreneurial – even if in a small way – I doubt we would today be living in one of the most intriguing and imposing houses in all Liverpool.

For decades there was rumour, gossip and debate amongst the multi–racial Liverpool 8 community where I grew up, that the house is the former hunting base for King John, the man who bestowed city status on Liverpool in 1207. On the streets we all believed that it still existed, straddling the borders of modern day Princes and Sefton parks. Now we have firm evidence that it incorporates the original building, known for centuries as the Higher Lodge.

The irony is that for 40 years investment banker Larry Rathbone lived there. His family had been a part of the fabric of Liverpool since the days of their anti–slavery campaigning ancestor, William Rathbone, and his equally socially aware daughter, Eleanor Rathbone. I suppose they would get a sense of satisfaction knowing that a descendant of slaves now owns the house.

It is one of Liverpool's most remarkable and best–kept historical secrets and we are looking after that legacy. And I am pleased in some ways that the waterfront where I played as a kid – as well as the cast iron shore at Dingle – is a World Heritage site. Now it is attractive rather than just a battered, derelict docks area.

But as I grew out of my teens the waterfront didn't really mean anything to me, or indeed most of the mixed race and black people of Liverpool. It still doesn't, really. Sure, it must have been fantastic to sail into Liverpool and, of course, I am here because my father did just that. However, there was nothing really for us in the centre of the city or at the Pier Head. Even though I am a proud Scouser, I don't actually feel involved with the high profile 'regeneration' of downtown Liverpool that has taken place in recent years.

That's a bit sad when you consider I live in a house that was perhaps where King John first considered elevating the small fishing port of Liverpool to a city in the 13th century.

*Beetham's 40-storey West Tower in Liverpool's Brook Street towers 300 feet above the waterfront and its Panoramic restaurant on the 34th floor claims to be the highest restaurant in the UK.*

*The Liverpool Marina at Coburg Wharf – home to the Liverpool Yacht Club that was founded in 1988. The marina is a haven for small boats, yachts and even grander luxury cruisers.*

*A view of Liverpool waterfront from Eastham; in the foreground a pontoon used for transferring crude oil from tankers to the Tranmere Oil Terminal.*

# Reflections on the Exoticism of Liverpool

David Fleming OBE

*Director, National Museums Liverpool*

FOR me the nature and character of this city is completely dependent on its river. This has been so right from the very early days, when nothing much really happened here, through the innovation of the 'wet dock' in the early 1700s and on to Liverpool's astonishing economic success, driven by the city's own people.

In most other cities the equivalent of our Museum of Liverpool would be concerned solely with the people, but in Liverpool you soon find yourself talking about a museum of the river, because so often the people stories emanate from it in some way or other. That might sound an obvious thing to say about a port, but in this city more than anywhere it is difficult to find any aspect of social life that was not integrally tied up with trade and the river. There is a turbulent and eccentric genius about the whole place, but you can never escape the waterfront.

From a cultural angle it is essential to understand why this city is like it is: don't just describe it as "edgy", or argumentative, or creative – these are just clichés unless you dig down and find an explanation for those characteristics. And the thing that people sometimes generated here by people who used the river. If there is really something in the water, it's what made people *entrepreneurial*.

What was it that made the Liverpool merchants of the early 18th century so successful? Why did they build a wet dock here on this little creek on the Mersey? After all, no one else had ever thought to tame a river in this way, to use technology to stop the ships keeling over as the tide came and went. Then there's the slave trade. Whatever our views today about the evils of the slave trade, consider it from a purely entrepreneurial perspective – Liverpool merchants saw others making money, so they took over the trade.

There is an entrepreneurialism here deep within the city's psyche that the modern world has lost sight of because the one way you wouldn't describe Liverpool between World War II and the 1990s was entrepreneurial. Yet, look a bit further back in time and you find these entrepreneurial and creative skills and a legacy of staggering wealth that contributed to the establishment of fabulous cultural institutions like St George's Hall and the Walker Art Gallery.

Although Liverpool's museums and galleries were awarded 'national' status in 1986 – because of the outstanding quality of the collections that were a direct consequence of Liverpool's merchant and trading capabilities

In many cities the merchant classes have been generous, but here there were more of them and they were richer than their contemporaries in other cities. Their philanthropic gestures were actually civic statements and expressions of success and wealth. It goes without saying that this wealth sat alongside almost biblical poverty – but that was the nature of industrial Britain.

Today our museums reflect the exoticism of Liverpool that was part and parcel of the life of the merchants and mariners who brought back strange and wonderful creatures, ideas and products from their travels: parrots, monkeys, textiles, great antiquities and other treasures, and later electric guitars and the latest sounds from America. Imagine what an exotic place Liverpool must have seemed when bananas were arriving for the first time!

Yet apart from the exoticism there is a huge and compelling people story. There were almost a million people here in that maritime heyday and, while many of them were connected to the river, there were other aspects of everyday life going on and not everyone went out on a boat. Our job in the Museum of Liverpool is to showcase the city's social history and popular culture, and that means telling the story of urban lifestyles.

The museum cost £71 million and it is Liverpool's first 21st century architectural masterpiece on the best

museum about any city in the world. People might ask why it's not in a bigger city: well it's not, because we had the spirit to go out and make it happen here in Liverpool! This city deserves a world-class museum to explore its extraordinary history. The only other cities in the world that have the capability to do what we are doing are the great capital cities; but you won't find anything like this museum in Berlin, Paris, Madrid or even New York.

Our museum is a result of contemporary thinking, about what a compelling city this is. It has travelled from obscurity, to unparalleled greatness, to almost terminal decline and now it is fighting to turn the corner again. And all the while the city's people were, and still are, producing this extraordinary creative output.

For a time there seemed to be no end to Liverpool's rise, when the sun never set on the British Empire. There was nowhere in the world that you couldn't find Liverpudlians or that Liverpool wasn't linked with; from Valparaiso and San Francisco, to Melbourne and Shanghai – every major port in Europe, Africa, the Americas, Asia, Australasia. Before World War I Liverpool and Manchester seemed to think that, between them, they could come to exert economic dominance over the whole country. There was a view that they could take over from London as the centre of finance, trade and wealth. Then

trouble well before the outbreak of World War II.

After the war Liverpool declined into one of the poorest cities in Europe, but managed to hang on through those dark years until it could revive itself.

Now as I witness that revival in the early years of the 21st century, somewhat later than in other northern post-industrial cities, my own belief is that the native entrepreneurialism is still here.

It is a growing city again, but in many ways it is still a difficult environment to make things happen in and I wonder if it is too early to judge whether Liverpool can get its 'mojo' back. But I happen to think that if Liverpool gets its cultural act together in the broadest sense of creativity, as well as the mainstream institutions in the arts, then there is a rosy future as a city: a place that other people – from across the world – will want to visit.

Personally, I am convinced that the core of Liverpool's revival is the cultural perspective; one which grows out of its entrepreneurialism. Our cultural assets are better than any other equivalent city in the UK. And there isn't a regional city in Europe that has a better cultural scene than we do here. The fact is that Liverpool is truly world class in one respect: culture. Culture, for me, is centre stage and is at the heart of our future as a competitive European city.

*A ferry completes a turn in the river on her way to Liverpool's landing stage, passing former dock sheds now transformed into a vibrant business park.*

*Residential living on one of the most sought after locations on the banks of the Mersey.*

# Chapter 8

*Otterspool to Hale*

*There is fun to be had sailing on the river but the Mersey is still a working waterway, even upstream, serving the ABP port at Garston and feeding into the Manchester Ship Canal at Ellesmere Port.*

POINTE DU SABLON
PORT AUX FRANCAIS

# That Feeling Called Home

**ZENG ZHI GAO**

*Deputy Chairman, Chinese Freemasons UK*
*and Liverpool restaurateur*

IT was early in 1945, when I was
barely 20 years of age, that I found
myself in the war–blitzed wasteland
that was Liverpool; a strangely exotic
and wildly foreign city to my eyes. I
spoke hardly any English apart from
a few random words I'd picked up in
Calcutta, from where I was transported
in a troopship – the *Empress of
Canada* – to join the vitally needed
pool of Chinese seamen who were to
help revive Britain's battle–scarred
merchant fleet.

Despite the situation, I was excited
to be in a country that I'd heard so much
about as a boy in my rural home close
to the Yangtze river in the province of
Sichuan.

Now I'm over 80 years of age
and have spent all of my adult life in
Liverpool. My old traditional Chinese
name was Chikhao Tseng but even
after living here for decades few British
friends can pronounce it. They call me

San, which I think is a very Liverpool
thing, and very friendly.

When I was 16 or 17 I was forced
to leave China and my family were
scattered far and wide because of the
Japanese war that had ravaged both
the cities and the vast countryside.
After Pearl Harbour and the American
intervention I was drafted into the
Chinese army, joining forces with the
British and American armies in the
struggle against Japan in Burma.

I was flown to Nepal for six months'
training. Then, with thousands of other
Chinese soldiers, in late 1941, I was
assigned to the Burmese front line,
where I spent 18 months in the heat of
battle. I was wounded twice and on the
second occasion, after being discharged
from a field hospital, discovered the
regiment had moved on.

I was quite weak and couldn't catch
them up and was finally invalided out
of the army because of my wounds.
Returning to China was still out of the
question and I was flown to Calcutta,
where I got a job as a waiter in a
Chinese restaurant. There I spotted an
advertisement for the British merchant
navy, which was looking for seamen.
I applied, although I didn't hold out
much hope as I was quite small. But, to
my utter surprise, I was accepted by the
Blue Funnel Line and shipped back to
England.

It was in many ways a journey into
the unknown but I was so grateful, if
somewhat apprehensive, to arrive in

Liverpool. Back in my hometown we
had often talked of this strange faraway
land called Britain, which we knew
of in historical terms because of the
Opium Wars of the 19th century. I never
imagined I would end up here.

These days I don't actually think
much about where I was born, although
I am, of course, very proud to be
Chinese; it's just that my family there
were dispersed many years ago. Indeed,
I regard Liverpool as my home, even if
my heart is still in China.

Once I had settled in Liverpool I got
a job and for 20 years I worked for the
Blue Funnel Line, traversing the globe as
a seaman and visiting most countries, but
always returning to Liverpool where my
British–born family live. My family are
fascinated by my story and I do feel lucky
that, out of the millions of Chinese people
who suffered from the wars and unrest of
that period, I survived and thrived.

After I was made redundant by
Blue Funnel Line, in 1965, I worked
part–time in a Chinese restaurant in
Manchester and as a casual docker on
the Liverpool and Birkenhead docks,
part of a shore gang.

At that time, in order to look after
my growing family I also opened a small
café on the Liverpool docksides. Today,
I am so pleased that *San's Café* is a
popular and regular haunt of so many
different kinds of customers: seafarers,
lorry drivers, dockworkers and the local
business community; all keen to sample
our blend of Chinese and British food.

Of course, I have noticed many
changes in Liverpool since I came here.
And I am really proud that the city has
taken off and that it has World Heritage
status, especially as that accolade was
announced in China and not that far
from where I was born. I suppose now
I am half Sichuanese and half Scouser.
And I'm delighted that Liverpool is
twinned with Shanghai.

I went back to China in 1958 looking
for my relatives and did find most of my
sisters and brothers, but the country
then underwent a turbulent time during
the Cultural Revolution and I didn't get
back again until 1982. Now I try to take
a trip to China every year. I am treated
like a VIP but have to admit that I am
always glad to return to Liverpool, where
everyone has been so kind to me.

*Liverpool's two famous cathedrals hem in the beer drinkers' own 'temple', the Cains Brewery building – in red brick – which was adapted from a former warehouse in 1902 and has become a 'household' name in the city and elsewhere.*

*Sailing on the wider reaches of the Mersey opposite the exclusive residential area of Cressington Park, which was once populated by ships' captains and maritime merchants who built themselves imposing mini–mansions.*

*It is early morning as a ferry sweeps along a calm river with ABP port at Garston as a backdrop.*

# Reflections on the Past

Louise O'Brien

*Manager, Historic Environment of Liverpool Project*
*English Heritage*

WHEN I was 13, I started a cleaning job to earn some pocket money. I cleaned an office in The Albany building on Old Hall Street in the historic commercial district of Liverpool – not that I knew it as that at the time. It was 1980.

Every Saturday morning I got the train into the city centre and walked from Moorfields station to the office. The streets were – are – extremely grand, the proportions monumental and the buildings densely packed and solid. Even at 13, I felt that this was an important place, somewhere of significance, although I couldn't articulate it then. But there was something missing. The area was a bit like the *Marie Celeste*, was a bit 'frayed' around the edges and, more to the point, where was everyone? Going down to the river Mersey after doing my cleaning

I'm like thousands upon thousands who've been born and bred in this most un–English *entrepôt* city; all the signs are there if you know what you're looking for. With a surname like O'Brien, there aren't any prizes for guessing where my ancestors are from or why they landed here. My maternal grandfather, who I never met, is buried at Montevideo in Uruguay in a merchant navy graveyard. I've a whole generation of relations who emigrated to Canada and Australia in the 1950s via the port of Liverpool, never to be seen again.

My paternal grandparents, amongst other things, ran a boarding house for travelling people, actors, performers and seamen. And, in an almost cartoonesque religious–identikit picture, I was christened a Unitarian, educated first at a Jewish school and then a Catholic convent. How very Liverpool.

The godfather of one of my sisters worked for Elder Dempster out of west Africa and we would visit him aboard ship whenever he docked in Liverpool. I loved listening to six or seven languages simultaneously amongst the crew, with the common linguistic denominator being a form of Pidgin. It always seemed like an exciting treat to sip soft drinks that you couldn't get in our local shops – a can of 'Ting' anyone? And I still have a Chinese vase that I somehow persuaded a couple of Nigerian crewmen to give me when I was about 10. However, enough with the rose–tinted nostalgia already.

Protected as I was to some extent from the vagaries of worklessness within the family, and the worst of its knock–on effects, I left Liverpool to study and then work and I came back in 1995. Again, I gravitated towards the river, daily, as a cycle route in and out of the city or just as a place to walk and look. The Albany on Old Hall Street was by then completely derelict but some of the iconic warehouses, in particular Jesse Hartley's Albert Dock set piece, were coming back into use on the waterfront as shops, bars and cultural centres. National Museums Liverpool was a key driver in this seismic shift in opinion that the dock buildings were valuable and should be kept and restored. There were definitely signs of change showing through the peeling façade of the city.

In this incredibly fast–moving world in which we live, glossy image making and global branding are *de rigueur*, but running alongside these is a deeply felt loss of 'sense of place' for many people. It can be difficult to retain a distinct identity, both for decision makers in the public and private sectors and, equally, for the people who live there. The characteristics which have made historic port cities such as Liverpool, New York, Lagos, Gdansk, Bombay, Shanghai and Marseille, amongst many others, different and set apart – cultural and ethnic diversity, being transportation centres for people and goods, the need to hustle and make a living, the physical infrastructure required to store, move, buy and sell goods, facing outwards instead of inwards – these all leave a wonderful but frustratingly difficult to define mark on the essence of a place.

What do you do then when that hustle and bustle of trade and mass–movement is quietened, that whole *raison d'être* not so clearly defined? What do people do, how will they live? In order to move forward, do we have to agree to live in a 'maritime theme park' preserved in aspic? Do we graciously acknowledge the passing of our function as a mercantile, maritime port city to the more generic 'waterfront city'? Perversely for one who barely considers herself English, I now work for English Heritage, specifically in Liverpool, and so have more reason than most perhaps to pose these fraught questions on a routine basis.

Liverpool has experienced an extraordinary period of accelerated change and development in the city centre and waterfront areas in recent years, and the whole city was placed under the microscope with the successful bid to become European Capital of Culture in 2008. Further attention was focused on Liverpool's city centre through 136 hectares of it being inscribed, in 2004, on the UNESCO World Heritage site list, which "confirms the exceptional and universal value of a cultural or natural site which requires protection for the benefit of all humanity". Liverpool was proposed for inscription as "the supreme example of a commercial port at the time of Britain's greatest global influence".

It is exciting and important to see how this reminds people of just how significant Liverpool was and is. It is especially poignant when in my mind's eye I picture how things were growing up in the 1980s with that overwhelming sense of civic decay and loss of cultural identity. More generally, the tide has changed in the culture and heritage sector as a more inclusive concept of what constitutes heritage has come to the fore. Industrial heritage, which Liverpool excels at, is now jostling for position with the more traditional view of 'stately homes' and grand houses and we start to see more modest building typologies such as warehouses, institutional buildings and the homes of ordinary people being recognised more fully.

As the statutory adviser to the government of England on the historic environment, English Heritage has a responsibility to help everyone care for the historic environment – this encompasses archaeology, historic built fabric, designed cultural landscapes, parks and gardens – as well as the headline historic houses and palaces. If pressed, many people would say that English Heritage exists to 'get in the way' of change or development. In fact, English Heritage works daily alongside developers, local government and others on the ground which is occupied equally by those opposed to any removal of historic fabric, those who have no attachment to heritage at all and those that believe that we deserve to keep the best of the old and place it alongside the best of the new. For some, English Heritage does not do enough to stop development and change, for others it does too much. In a city like Liverpool, that debate is continuous and lively.

While Liverpool has been suffering from the capricious tides of change over the past century, other places have risen in prominence and have successfully begun the process of reinvention more quickly. At some level, decisions have to be made about what, if anything, is retained from the past; cultural and historical revisionism is not an option. Embarrassment about or disinterest in a period of history, for example the pre–eminence of Liverpool in the creation and development of the transatlantic slave trade, or the time in the 1980s when monumental buildings and other cultural collections were at real risk of being completely obliterated – some would say that they were destroyed anyway – shouldn't stop that story being told now or in the future. In a hundred or 500 years' time, people will judge us in the same way that we judge our predecessors, on the basis of what a society chooses to keep.

The challenge remains in what we *add* to the story rather than what we take away. If I could put some buildings or structures back in Liverpool that have been lost, they would be the Liverpool Overhead Railway – the 'Dockers' Umbrella' as it was fondly called – the trams, the original St John's Market, the original Clayton Square and the Sailors' Home. I wish someone had kept just one of the true court dwellings in the city; tiny, dingy, few windows, no light, cramped and unsanitary but lived in by such a huge number of Liverpool people and where my paternal grandfather was born in 1881.

Which brings me back to my original point; it is not possible for me to separate myself and my job from Liverpool – an historic port city on the edge.

I was visiting a friend not long ago who lives in The Albany building on Old Hall Street. It's been beautifully and sympathetically restored and brought into use as residential accommodation. Good use has been made of the huge windows, the corridors are bright with crisp lighting; it is as symmetrical as I remember it. It's probably just me, but I still preferred it when, on Saturdays, I had the whole slightly tatty building to myself and I wandered along the elegant stone halls and cantilevered staircases singing to myself, having peeped through the post box of every single office on the way as I left for home.

'The characteristics which have made historic port cities such as Liverpool, New York, Lagos, Gdansk, Bombay, Shanghai and Marseille, amongst many others, different and set apart... these all leave  a wonderful - but frustratingly difficult to define - mark on the essence of a place'

As the river rolls inexorably towards its widest point at Hale and opposite Ince marshes – the largest wildfowl reserve in Britain – a rural mood seemingly embraces the land on either side. Yet across the river the control tower of Liverpool John Lennon Airport declares that such tranquillity is only fleeting.

*The monochrome reaches of the Mersey at Hale are filled with the sound of wildfowl and bird song and the rustling of wind in the reeds, along with the waving ears of corn in the nearby fields, or the rush of the tide which runs fast along the deep channels along this part of the river. It has an almost mystical mood where once, perhaps, 'Lord Log' reigned amidst the mudflats and sandbars.*

# The Wrap From Over The Mersey Wall

WHEN I was a young kid, my father and I were standing on the banks of the River Mersey under the Liver Birds. Pointing across the enormous, Amazonian River to the Wirral, I asked: "What's that over there, dad?"

Having tended his cotton boss's gardens in Heswall on the Wirral for extra money when he was young, he replied: "That's OVER THE WATER son". Unattainable....a place that Liverpool working class families like us could only dream about.

Well here I am, sixty years later, writing about the munificence of the Mersey in... you guessed it...Heswall on the Wirral...the Beverley Hills of Liverpool! Not only that, they've made that scruffy Liverpool lad the *Cultural Ambassador for Wirral, where it's fortuitous that I now point out to visitors that the best shots of Liverpool and its World Heritage Waterfront are from 'over the water' on the Wirral.

Over the many years travelling with Scaffold, plus lately as a photographer – just returned from the Rock and Roll Hall of Fame in Ohio, where my *Mike McCartney's Liverpool Life* exhibition has transferred from the Smithsonian Institution in Washington DC – my Liverpool accent has watered down to become more Mid Mersey than Mid Atlantic, but at least I can claim to personally 'know' the River Mersey.

**MIKE MCCARTNEY**

*Wirralian Scouser*

As a family we used to paddle in its often freezing waters at the mouth of the Mersey in New Brighton by Fort Perch Rock, and later on my school mates and I would sag off from Stockton Wood Road School in Speke on hot summer days – in rest periods of course, kids – to stroll through the rhododendron woods – now the John Lennon Airport – to the back of Speke Hall where we would skinny dip in the Mersey...it was that clean!

Thankfully the River Mersey is slowly returning to its former glory and with global warming and the new Liverpool Museum at the Pierhead joining Unesco's World Heritage Site, like the Pyramids and the Taj Mahal, a little bird tells me that we'll all be able to dive bomb from its top into an azure blue, lukewarm Mersey and swim through schools of rainbow coloured, tropical fish to small palm tree islands dotted around the river...and I actually believe that little (Liver) bird.

So, finally, where does Mike McCartney stand with regards Liverpool, the Mersey and the Wirral? Born and brought up in Liverpool on its old fashioned right and wrong ethics, standards and quick witted rules – and even given an Honorary Fellowship by Liverpool John Moore's University – in my heart I'm a Scouser.

But I've lived on the Wirral for twice as long, and even been 'Culturally Ambassadored' by them. So, here I am, stuck in the middle of 'over the water'...with best views of BOTH sides...in fact I stand in the middle of the Mersey...and I've not sunk yet!

*\* Sorry, we were never scruffy...our mum was a health visitor*

*Hale lighthouse at the farthest inland stretch of the river Mersey. Erected in 1906, it is 45 feet in height atop red sandstone cliffs and its beam could apparently be seen from 40 miles away. It was decommissioned in 1958 and the main lamplight is preserved in the Maritime Museum at Albert Dock in Liverpool.*

GUY WOODLAND was born in Karachi and has lived and worked extensively in Australia, Pakistan, Ethiopia, Portugal, Brazil and the UK. He studied at Blackpool and Fylde College, earning a diploma in professional photography. He owns liverpoolphotos.com, an online global picture resource and operates internationally as a photographer

He is co–founder of *Cities500* and has published a range of books that includes the popular photographic studies: *The Life of Chester, The Life of the Gateway Theatre* and *Life of Liverpool* along with

LEW BAXTER is co–founder of *Cities500* and has 40 years experience as a writer and journalist, variously with the *Sunday Times, Daily Telegraph*, the *Scotsman*, the *Daily Post* and the *Sunday Mirror* in the UK. He has also written for *China Daily*, the *Shanghai Star* and the *Hong Kong Standard* amongst others.

He spent a number of years in China in the 1990s where he was latterly bureau chief of *Sino Media Limited*, following a period as Far East bureau chief for the USA owned *Phillips Publishing International Group*. At one stage he was consultant English language

*Mersey Mouth*

'Out of the mouth of the Mersey:
Tall ships and tall stories
Songs, slaves, poems and pig iron
Cargoes of dreams and laughter'

*Roger McGough*


*Reflections on the Waterfront*

'Two green birds with a
brown ribbon flowing forever,
the Waterfront is
Liverpool's front door'

*Brian Jacques*